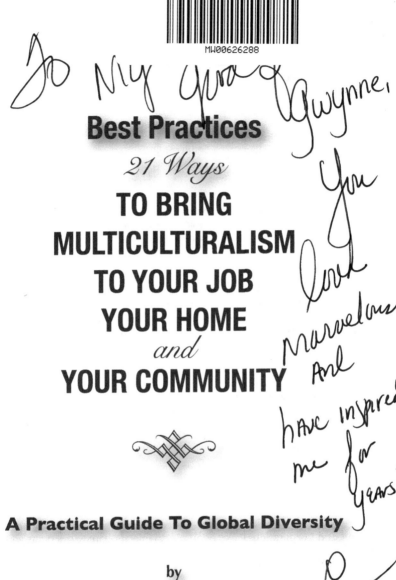

Best Practices

21 Ways
TO BRING
MULTICULTURALISM
TO YOUR JOB
YOUR HOME
and
YOUR COMMUNITY

A Practical Guide To Global Diversity

by
Carole Copeland Thomas, MBA CDMP

Milormic Press
Lakeville, Massachusetts, USA

Handwritten inscription: To My Dear Gwynne, You love Marvelous And have inspired me for years!

9/16/12

First Edition
Copyright ©2012 - Carole Copeland Thomas
All Rights Reserved

ISBN 978-0-9741283-1-3

Publisher's Cataloging-in-Publication Data
(Prepared by Cassidy Cataloguing Services, Inc.)

Thomas, Carole Copeland.

> Best practices: 21 ways to bring multcuturalism to your job, your home
> and your community : a practical guide to global diversity / by Carole
> Copeland Thomas. -- 1st ed. -- Lakeville, Mass. : Milormic Press, c2012.

>> p. ; cm.

>> ISBN: 978-0-9741283-1-3
>> Includes bibliographical references.
>> Summary: A practical guide for those with a working knowledge of
>> diversity who need resources and information to craft an advocacy
>> campaign of their own.--Publisher.

>> 1. Multiculturalism--Handbooks, manuals, etc. 2. Cultural pluralism--
>> Handbooks, manuals, etc. 3. Diversity in the workplace--Handbooks,
>> manuals, etc. 4. Equality. 5. Self-perception. I. Title. II. Title: 21 ways to
>> bring multiculturalism to your job, your home and your community.

>> HM1271 . T46 2012
>> 305.8--dc23   1208

Schools and Corporations: This book is available at quantity discounts with bulk purchases for educational or business use. For more information please contact the publisher at the address below.

Milormic Press • (508) 947-5755
6 Azel Road • Lakeville, MA 02347

Editor: Nathine Washington
Printed in the United States of America
King Printing (www.kingprinting.com)

Table Of Contents

TABLE OF CONTENTS

Dedicated To

My Children

My Grandchildren

My Family

and

In Loving Memory

Of My Son

Mickarl D. Thomas, Jr.

Forward

I have known Carole for nearly 20 years. We met in the mid-1990s through our trade organization, the National Speakers Association. Our friendship and business relationships have deepened through the years to collaborating on projects, speaking engagements and our Ebony Speakers' mastermind group.

She is a success story that is known around the globe if you follow her on LinkedIn, Facebook and Twitter. She is a professional speaker, trainer, facilitator, executive coach, author, mother, grandmother and a dear friend to so many people globally. Carole's voice is strong and powerful throughout and her wealth of talent, skills and abilities are crafted in this book entitled, Best Practices: 21 Ways To Bring Multiculturalism To Your Job Your Home and Your Community. She is very bold, courageous and delivers unique tips that will move the reader to action.

Over 25 years, Carole has learned how to deliver a solid message in the business community on the importance of multiculturalism. I had the opportunity and privilege to support and participate in the first Multiculturalism Symposium Series Conference in October 2008 in Boston, Massachusetts. You have to know Carole on a personal and professional level to understand that when she put her mind to something as a friend, business colleague, neighbor, church member, professor or student you are counted in the vision. Carole creates magic with every business endeavor that you want to be actively involved in on the journey.

The book artfully walks you through the journey with understanding relationship between multiculturalism and diversity. Best Practices: 21 Ways To Bring Multiculturalism To Your

Job Your Home and Your Community is an excellent book filled with tips that teaches how to move from diversity to inclusion. This book provides education, awareness and practical tips to anyone who aspires to create a productive work environment that is both diverse and genuinely inclusive.

The reader will move closer to the ideas of living in a harmonious society. The first chapter reminds me of the passage of Scripture in Acts: 17:26 where God "hath made of one blood all nations of men for to dwell on all the face of the earth." (KJV)

Then we move on to defining diversity as understanding, appreciating and ultimately managing difference and similarities at the same time. The simplicity of the definition deals more with acceptance of reality. Diversity helps develop the understanding that some structures must be recognized as impediments to creating a true multicultural participation in society as a whole. Who we are is so much more than our gender, age, race ethnicity and other observable traits. You can't stop there. Diversity includes our education, marital status; socio-economic status, abilities, language and sexual orientation. Our ability to accept all people for who they are even when they are different from us, shows that we are people who are comfortable and secure in our own identity, values and beliefs.

The book is cleverly crafted to create a process to unlearn all of the mistakes of the past. The author challenges the leadership roles in organizations to understand that there must be buy-in to change the behavior from exclusion to inclusion.

Diversity is not a dress rehearsal on your job. It represents the landscape of our community as human beings. We should want to celebrate, understand and appreciate the difference and similarities first taught in your home. I believe this book is a roadmap to start the journey at your job, your home and your community.

I hope that every CEO, Board of Director, Community Leader will read this book for a better understanding of why diversity is so important to the success of your organization. Every industry leader should want to encourage their managers and supervisors to invest in this book and connect with this global diversity leader at www.mssconnect.com. Enjoy the experience.

Debra W. Gould

President & CEO
Debra Gould & Associates, Inc.
www.gouldassoc.com

Introduction

Multiculturalism and diversity are words that are part of my DNA. For the past 25 years I have worked with large and small companies and organizations helping to enhance the personal and professional potential of people from different backgrounds, ethnicities and races. The work has been richly rewarding, filled with new possibilities and satisfies my need to bring people together, no matter how difficult the challenge.

I have traveled and spoken in most of the states in the US and have a deep yearning to visit every country beyond the six I have visited that help validate my claim as an "international" speaker and trainer. My ultimate quest is to bring people together throughout the world.

That is why this book is so important. **Best Practices: 21 Ways To Bring Multiculturalism To Your Job Your Home And Your Community** is practical guide for those with a working knowledge of diversity who need resources and information to craft an advocacy campaign of their own. This book has been years in the making and is only the first of several I plan on writing on the subject.

I am a big believer that the ultimate sustainable success of multiculturalism and diversity will depend on the personal commitment of individuals who want to see real change in our societies. I call them "Diversity Champions" in my last chapter. These are real people who need practical resources and a game plan to navigate the uncertainties and sensitive nature of cross cultural relationships. This book is designed to give useful tips, suggestions, websites, and information to build a credible portfolio for managing this process both on and off the job.

From enhanced diversity training programs, to knowledge transfer, to organizing a family reunion, there is something in this book for everyone to use.

As an American, my point of reference is US based. However, over the past ten years, through technology and travel my world has become internationally focused. I no longer believe that domestic diversity in the US will help us reach our goals. We have to employ a global strategy to fully serve as an inclusive worldwide body of Diversity Champions. It is in this spirit that this book has been written.

A few years ago I started the **Multicultural Symposium Series** (MSS) (www.mssconnect.com). It is a face to face, online and broadcasting community designed to further the advancement of worldwide multiculturalism and global diversity. MSS connects with humanity, and this book is an extension of that endeavor. MSS held its first three conferences in partnership with Bentley University. The University of Massachusetts-Boston has partnered with MSS for the remaining conferences held to date.

I encourage you to read this book with pen in hand. Highlight the chapters that speak to your needs. Make notes on how you will achieve your goals, once you create that personal game plan that will take you on your global diversity journey. Use this book as a personal guide. Then share its value with your friends, family members, colleagues, classmates and students.

This book is also about personal empowerment. My mantra has always been, *"Empowerment Begins When You Believe In Yourself."* I hope you will use this book to take on the world by empowering your spirit to connect with all of the diverse people who come into your life.

Carole Copeland Thomas

Chapter 1.

Why Multiculturalism???

The plurality of the world compels us to learn, adjust, modify, and expand our knowledge base to accommodate the faces of change we see every day. No longer is it acceptable to just "tolerate" the differences in our daily lives. We must integrate those differences and similarities into a personal routine that feels comfortable in our homes, communities, our houses of worship, our neighborhoods, and on our jobs.

I have spent nearly 25 years fully exploring difference. It's been a pioneering adventure with some rewards and many challenges. I have seen the words change from integration to inclusion. From ending racial discrimination to celebrating diversity. I have seen compliance in affirmative action benefit some ethnic and gender groups, while leaving other groups struggling for higher stakes in socio-economic development. Words like multiculturalism, global diversity and inclusion have grown up to mean different things to different segments of our society. For some, the words are a breakthrough in a nationwide dialogue long overdue in the "land of the free." For others the words represent division, discourse, and polarization too distasteful for polite society to discuss in public or in private.

My vision is to allow all of these voices to be heard in a world that provides the format and parameters that enables discussions and debates of all sizes to occur in countries around the planet. As an American I want my own country to lead the way, set the example and frame some of the discussions. However, as a global citizen I want the people world to fully participate in these discussions where multiculturalism captures the imagination of the young and old wherever they happen to live.

Multiculturalism Vs. Diversity

Multiculturalism represents the landscape of our community as human beings. It's a bigger concept than diversity because its very meaning requires an open platform for embracing multiple cultures, ethnic groups and ideologies within a society. Multicultural means many cultures operating in the same space. America, like other countries, is multicultural because different cultural groups maintain a meaningful co-existence within the span of 50 states. Even though there are decades of history where oppression, racism, discrimination and legislative restrictions affected one ethnic group over another, the cultural coexistence remains a vital link to our identity as Americans.

Multiculturalism demands that you coexist with others. In a truly multicultural society, one cultural group does not dominate another. The abundance theory is the prevailing rule, where society's output is big enough for all of our cultures and ethnicities to be represented in an equally respectable manner.

We seem to fully embrace multiculturalism in food. Food seems to be one of the few cultural centers that stands on its own. Visit any mall or shopping center in any city or town and the food courts are populated by people of all walks of life. From soul food to cajun cooking, to chinese cuisine to Indian vegetarian dishes, a typical food court presents the best argument that cultural pluralism can yield good value to any consumer's taste buds.

On the other hand, some aspects of multiculturalism are closely guarded and tolerated only to a point. It's fascinating to watch professionals in the workplace celebrate the worthiness of multiculturalism on the job. One would think that the level of commitment to cross cultural causes would get packed up and taken straight home to share, just like that leftover shrimp fried rice gets taken home after the party at work has ended. Instead, far too often you witness the reinforcement of cultural silos as employees head to cars, buses and trains to take them back to their neighborhoods that are all White, all Black, all Hispanic, or mostly Asian. The social conformity of our neighborhoods provide the greatest opportunity for us to breakthrough our comfort zones, venture out, and live among other cultures. That, my friends, we'll save for another book. It represents one of the central frontiers of true multiculturalism.

Diversity is an important byproduct of multiculturalism. It speaks to the segmentation of our societies and frames the very categories that define who we are as individuals and members of specific groups or cultural components.

I define Diversity from this perspective:

Diversity is understanding, appreciating and ultimately managing difference and similarities at the same time.

The emphasis is on the word AND. Diversity looks at both difference AND similarities, with one not being more important than the other. That's where most people make a mistake by focusing on either one's difference or one's similarities without realizing that BOTH are in operation at the same time. For example, as an African American female, when speaking at conferences and meetings, I am accustomed to being "the only one," that is, the only person of color either attending the meeting or speaking at the meeting. To focus on my difference from the rest of the conference attendees is only embracing half the experience. The other half recognizes that there are personal values, educational experiences, regional interests and industry issues that I share as similar points of intersection with those attending the same meeting. To just focus on my ethnic difference cancels out the rich value of those similarities of which I share in common with others.

Okay, let me explain it another way. Some years ago I traveled to Kenya for the first time. It was the trip of a lifetime for me. The minute I stepped off that airplane, pulled out my American passport and presented it to the customs officer at the Nairobi, Kenya Airport, my differences AND similarities were on full display with every other American on that plane. Some of the passengers had Black skin like mine. My travel mates (now known as the Kenya Sistahs - www.kenyasistahs.org) were also African American females. Some of the passengers were White Americans, Hispanics, while others were Asian Americans. There were Europeans, Asians and Africans on the plane, too. So the differences were on full display from ethnicity, gender and socioeconomic class. However, the similarities also represented this collection of travelers. I held an American passport, as did many others on the plane. And meeting other Americans on that maiden voyage trip to mother Africa was so very exciting, since we were all thousands of miles away from home, and it was comforting to connect with expatriates from the States.

In diversity work, the similarities are as important as the differences.

Similarities are on equal footing with differences. That is so important to remember since there is an incorrect assumption that diversity is polarizing because it only focuses on differences at the expense of similarities.

You see it in families all the time. Brothers and sisters with the same biological parents, yet their values and opinions are as different as night and day. I see it in my own adult daughters, Michelle and Lorna. Their political, spiritual and economic opinions are very similar. However, their work habits, approach to preparation and personalities completely different.

The same is true for extended families, members of associations and corporate colleagues. The differences should be valued with the same level of importance as the similarities. They represent a different slice of the diversity equation.

Common US Based Diversity Categories

Class/Household Income/Economic Status

African American/Black

Biracial/Multicultural

White Americans/European Americans/Caucasians

Hispanic/Latino/Latina

Asian American/Pacific Islander

Native American/American Indian

Arab Americans

Sexual Orientation: (LGBT) Lesbian, Gay, Bisexual, Transgender

Heterosexual

Metrosexual

Gender/Male-Female Issues

Persons With Disabilities

Age Issues - Multigenerational Issues

Religion

Education

Political Beliefs

Nationality

Physical Size

Work - Managerial Styles

The Journey Starts With Understanding The Relationship Between Multiculturalism and Diversity

These definitions for multiculturalism and diversity represent the start of our journey down the road of discovering 21 ways to bring multiculturalism into your way of thinking. It's from that platform that I have launched a practical and easily achievable method of finding ways to make multiculturalism a regular part of your life. Diversity is the natural byproduct. All that is left is your willingness to explore suggestions and ideas that will help you demonstrate your commitment to these important global concepts. Some may be completely familiar to you, while others may take some time to embrace. Wherever you start, know that undertaking diversity and multiculturalism takes time. It doesn't happen overnight. Like fine wine aging in oak barrels, the longer you explore and try out these important concepts, the better you'll get in time. Understanding and exploring your own relationship with diversity and multiculturalism will bring you closer to the connection you have with people across the street and across the globe.

Good luck, welcome to the world of multiculturalism, and enjoy the journey.

This book may use the words multicultural and diversity interchangeably.

Remember that **multiculturalism** represents the global landscape of cultures all over the world. **Diversity** is its byproduct that categorizes groups of people while equally managing differences and similarities at the same time.

The terms are interrelated and often used interchangeably. This book will also follow that pattern of using multiculturalism and diversity without minimizing the essence of their individual meaning.

Chapter 2

Tip #1: Design and Create a Diversity Calendar For Your Workplace

Years ago when I served as the diversity consultant for The TJX Companies (parent company to TJ Maxx, Marshalls, AJ Wright and Home Goods) the company took great pride in producing a high quality calendar for all of their employees. I remember working with the corporate steering committee as they carefully explored each and every design option for each given year. It took months of preparation, and was a costly endeavor, but well worth it. One year they featured recipes of selected employees. Another year they featured clothing and fashion garments from around the world. Each calendar represented the "fabric" of the organization displayed in a graphically appealing way that helped connect the employees to the company in a personal and meaningful way.

In the case of The TJX Companies, the Diversity Calendar was a budget line item that demonstrated a tangible way to showcase the company's commitment to the cause. Yes, there were costs associated with designing, approving, printing and distributing the calendar to thousands of employees, Nevertheless,YOUR company calendar can be created in a cost effective manner suitable to your budget parameters.

Make Sure Your Company Calendar Symbolizes Your Workforce

Make sure you get buy-in from your employees to ensure that your calendar project best represent your workforce. The more employees and staff members identify with the multicultural calendar, the more successful it will be throughout the year. If you have a calendar committee or special project team to design and develop the calendar, include key employees, managers, supervisors and executives on the design team.

You might have staff members born outside of the country who have special connections to holidays like Boxing Day (December 26th in the United Kingdom) or Jamhuri Day on December 12th (Independence Day) in Kenya or the two day celebration of Holi in India during the month of March.

Search The Internet For Worldwide Holidays

Technology makes it so easy now to research different holidays to include on your calendar. Here is a list of websites that offer dates and descriptions of various cultural holidays around the world.

Multicultural Calendar sponsored by Dominion Power Company

http://www.dom.com/about/education/culture/index.jsp

University of Kansas Medical Center Diversity Calendar

http://www3.kumc.edu/diversity/ethnic_relig/ethnic.html

University of Rochester Multicultural Calendar

http://www.rochester.edu/diversity/calendar.html

Include Workforce Birthdays If Appropriate

What better way to recognize your employees, colleagues, and staff than creating a special internal calendar that lists the birth dates of each employee in your organization. This may work more effectively as an online calendar printed out monthly to allow for staff changes and company updates. The recognition will encourage staff members to exchange birthday cards, greetings, and arrange for parties or other social gatherings for special birthdays for the "employee of the month." Ethnic and other cultural special dates should also be included in the workforce calendar.

Create A Special Calendar For Client Gifts

Perhaps there is a special relationship your company has with certain clients. Or you are "courting" a prized prospect through a lengthy series of discussions and presentations. Why not create a specialized print or online calendar with historical facts specific to your prospect? Or determine the favorite sport or travel destination of your prospect and create a specialize calendar showcasing cultural highlights they would appreciate?

For example, your number one client company enjoys taking their sales force to Jamaica following a sales contest for vacation, sports and recreation. Why not research the history of the island, when it gained independence and the phenomenal rise of the Jamaican bobsled (bobsleigh) team that competed in the Winter Olympics?

Sell A Special Version To Customers

You can take the entire multicultural calendar concept up one level and sell a high end print version to your customer or client base. Unless you're mass producing thousands or millions of your calendar at a reduced price ($10 - $20), most likely you will produce a few hundred/thousand at a higher price point of $20 - $25.

Calendar projects need to be designed and researched between January and June or the previous year. The calendar is then printed between July and September (often offshore in China to reduce costs for a full color calendar). It is then sold between October and January. The calendar can then be reduced in price after January to clear your inventory as you prepare for next year's calendar.

Tight Budget? Create An Online Calendar

Why not put all of your energy in research, design an visually strong calendar and debut it online at your company website? That is what Dominion has done in website referenced above by creating a comprehensive online calendar for all to use. It becomes cost effective for your company or organization and a traffic builder to your website.

An online website can also be changed, modified, or enhanced regularly by your calendar committee to keep it relevant and up-to-date as a viable cultural resource.

Chapter 3

Tip #2: Display The National Flags Of Your Employees

The world is so interconnected these days that large and small organizations can boast of employees who originate from different parts of the world. For a decade I served as the diversity consultant for Mattapan Community Health Center, a vibrant health center in the heart of urban Boston. With nearly one hundred on staff, the center's employee base represented at lease five different countries in North America, the Caribbean Islands, Central America, and Africa. It is common for companies and organizations in urban centers throughout the world to have employees whose ethnic origins are well outside the borders of your country.

Why not honor their heritage by displaying flags in your lobby, your front entrance, or your cafeteria?

I have worked with some wise clients who visibly display the flag of every country representing the country of origin of their staff members. Usually the flag displays are placed in a large hall, foyer, or dramatically displayed outside at the front entrance of the visitor entrance. It provides a warm, symbolic, and colorful welcome to all who visit the organization and visibly announces the respect the employer has for those who labor in their vineyard.

Flag displays can also be used with clients, to showcase the geographic representation of a company's product or service reach beyond their natural boundaries.

Displaying The American Flag vs. Other Flags

Some countries, like Kenya, have restrictions on what government objects and symbols can and cannot be photographed. Use this information as an opportunity to learn more about, let's say the Kenyan flag or Canadian flag and compare the differences.

Here is information from The Flag Code Title 4, United States Code, Chapter 1 that gives the correct positioning and placement of the American flag. This passage is lengthy, but why not turn this passage into a lively discussion, comparing the "rules" for displaying the American flag with the "rules" of flags in other countries?

Here it is:

 As adopted by the National Flag Conference, Washington, D.C., June 14-15, 1923, and Revised and Endorsed by the Second National Flag Conference, Washington, D.C., May 15, 1924. Revised and adopted at P.L. 623, 77th Congress, Second Session, June 22, 1942; as Amended by P.L. 829, 77th Congress, Second Session, December 22, 1942; P.L. 107 83rd Congress, 1st Session, July 9, 1953; P.L. 396, 83rd Congress, Second Session, June 14, 1954; P.L. 363, 90th Congress, Second Session, June 28, 1968; P.L. 344, 94th Congress, Second Session, July 7, 1976; P.L. 322, 103rd Congress, Second Session, September 13, 1994; P.L. 225, 105th Congress, Second Session, August 12, 1998; P.L. 80, 106th Congress, First Session, October 25, 1999; P.L. 110-41, 110th Congress, First Session, June 29, 2007; P.L. 110-181, 110th Congress, Second Session, January 28, 2008; P.L. 110-239, 110th Congress, Second Session, June 3, 2008, P.L. 110-417, 110th Congress, Second Session, October 14,

2008; and P.L. 111-41, 111th Congress, First Session, July 27, 2009.

4. Pledge of Allegiance to the flag; manner of delivery

The Pledge of Allegiance to the Flag, ''I pledge allegiance to the Flag of the United States of America, and to the Republic for which it stands, one Nation under God, indivisible, with liberty and justice for all.'', should be rendered by standing at attention facing the flag with the right hand over the heart. When not in uniform men should remove their headdress with their right hand and hold it at the left shoulder, the hand being over the heart. Persons in uniform should remain silent, face the flag, and render the military salute.

5. Display and use of flag by civilians; codification of rules and customs; definition

The following codification of existing rules and customs pertaining to the display and use of the flag of the United States of America is established for the use of such civilians or civilian groups or organizations as may not be required to conform with regulations promulgated by one or more executive departments of the Government of the United States. The flag of the United States for the purpose of this chapter shall be defined according to sections 1 and 2 of this title and Executive Order 10834 issued pursuant thereto.

6. Time and occasions for display

(a) It is the universal custom to display the flag only from sunrise to sunset on buildings and on stationary flagstaffs in the open. However, when a patriotic effect is desired, the flag may be displayed 24 hours a day if properly illuminated during the hours of darkness.

(b) The flag should be hoisted briskly and lowered ceremoniously.

(c) The flag should not be displayed on days when the weather is inclement, except when an all weather flag is displayed.

(d) The flag should be displayed on all days, especially on New Year's Day, January 1; Inauguration Day, January 20; Martin Luther King, Jr.'s birthday, the third Monday in January; Lincoln's Birthday, February 12; Washington's Birthday, third Monday in February; Easter Sunday (variable); Mother's Day, second Sunday in May; Armed Forces Day, third Saturday in May; Memorial Day (half-staff until noon), the last Monday in May; Flag Day, June 14; Father's Day, third Sunday in June; Independence Day, July 4; National Korean War Veterans Armistice Day, July 27; Labor Day, first Monday in September; Constitution Day, September 17; Columbus Day, second Monday in October; Navy Day, October 27; Veterans Day, November 11; Thanksgiving Day, fourth Thursday in November; Christmas Day, December 25; and such other days as may be proclaimed by the President of the United States; the birthdays of States (date of admission); and on State holidays.

(e) The flag should be displayed daily on or near the main administration building of every public institution.

(f) The flag should be displayed in or near every polling place on election days.

(g) The flag should be displayed during school days in or near every schoolhouse.

7. Position and manner of display

The flag, when carried in a procession with another flag or flags, should be either on the marching right; that is, the flag's own right, or, if there is a line of other flags, in front of the center of that line.

(a) The flag should not be displayed on a float in a parade except from a staff, or as provided in subsection (i) of this section.

(b) The flag should not be draped over the hood, top, sides, or back of a vehicle or of a railroad train or a boat. When the flag is displayed on a motorcar, the staff shall be fixed firmly to the chassis or clamped to the right fender.

(c) No other flag or pennant should be placed above or, if on the same level, to the right of the flag of the United States of America, except during church services conducted by naval chaplains at sea, when the church pennant may be flown above the flag during church services for the personnel of the Navy. No person shall display the flag of the United Nations or any other national or international flag equal, above, or in a position of superior prominence or honor to, or in place of, the flag of the United States at any place within the United States or any Territory or possession thereof: Provided, That nothing in this section shall make unlawful the continuance of the practice heretofore followed of displaying the flag of the United Nations in a position of superior prominence or honor, and other national flags in positions of equal prominence or honor, with that of the flag of the United States at the headquarters of the United Nations.

(d) The flag of the United States of America, when it is displayed with another flag against a wall from crossed staffs, should be on the right, the flag's own right, and its staff should be in front of the staff of the other flag.

(e) The flag of the United States of America should be at the center and at the highest point of the group when a number of flags of States or localities or pennants of societies are grouped and displayed from staffs.

(f) When flags of States, cities, or localities, or pennants of societies are flown on the same halyard with the flag of the United States, the latter should always be at the peak. When the flags are flown from adjacent staffs, the flag of the United States should be hoisted first and lowered last. No such flag or pennant may be placed above the flag of the United States or to the United States flag's right.

(g) When flags of two or more nations are displayed, they are to be flown from separate staffs of the same height. The flags should be of approximately equal size.

International usage forbids the display of the flag of one nation above that of another nation in time of peace.

(h) When the flag of the United States is displayed from a staff projecting horizontally or at an angle from the window sill, balcony, or front of a building, the union of the flag should be placed at the peak of the staff unless the flag is at half-staff. When the flag is suspended over a sidewalk from a rope extending from a house to a pole at the edge of the sidewalk, the flag should be hoisted out, union first, from the building.

(i) When displayed either horizontally or vertically against a wall, the union should be uppermost and to the flag's own right, that is, to the observer's left. When displayed in a window, the flag should be displayed in the same way, with the union or blue field to the left of the observer in the street.

(j) When the flag is displayed over the middle of the street, it should be suspended vertically with the union to the north in an east and west street or to the east in a north and south street.

(k) When used on a speaker's platform, the flag, if displayed flat, should be displayed above and behind the speaker. When displayed from a staff in a church or public auditorium, the flag of the United States of America should hold the position of superior prominence, in advance of the audience, and in the position of honor at the clergyman's or speaker's right as he faces the audience. Any other flag so displayed should be placed on the left of the clergyman or speaker or to the right of the audience.

(l) The flag should form a distinctive feature of the ceremony of unveiling a statue or monument, but it should never be used as the covering for the statue or monument.

(m) The flag, when flown at half-staff, should be first hoisted to the peak for an instant and then lowered to the half-staff position. The flag should be again raised to the peak before it is lowered for the day. On Memorial Day the flag should be displayed at half-staff until noon only, then raised to the top of the staff. By order of the President, the flag shall be flown at half-staff upon the death of principal figures of the United States Government and the Governor of a State, territory, or possession, as a mark of respect to their memory. In the event of the death of other officials or foreign dignitaries, the flag is to be displayed at half-staff according to Presidential instructions or orders, or in accordance with recognized customs or practices not inconsistent with law. In the event of the death of a present or former official of the government of any State, territory, or possession of the United States or the death of a member of the Armed Forces from any State, territory, or possession who dies while serving on active duty, the Governor of that State, territory, or possession may proclaim that the National flag shall be flown at half-staff and the same authority is provided to the Mayor of the District of Columbia with respect to present or former officials of the District of Columbia and members of the Armed Forces from the District of Columbia. When the Governor of a State, territory, or possession, or the Mayor of the District of Columbia, issues a proclamation under the preceding sentence that the National flag be flown at half-staff in that State, territory, or possession or in the District of Columbia because of the death of a member of the Armed Forces, the National flag flown at any Federal installation or facility in the area covered by that proclamation shall be flown at half-staff consistent with that proclamation. The flag shall be flown at half-staff 30 days from the death of the President or a former President; 10 days from the day of death of the Vice President, the Chief Justice or a retired Chief Justice of the United States, or the Speaker of the

House of Representatives; from the day of death until interment of an Associate Justice of the Supreme Court, a Secretary of an executive or military department, a former Vice President, or the Governor of a State, territory, or possession; and on the day of death and the following day for a Member of Congress. The flag shall be flown at half-staff on Peace Officers Memorial Day, unless that day is also Armed Forces Day. As used in this subsection -

(1) the term "half-staff" means the position of the flag when it is one-half the distance between the top and bottom of the staff;

(2) the term "executive or military department" means any agency listed under sections 101 and 102 of title 5, United States Code; and

(3) the term "Member of Congress" means a Senator, a Representative, a Delegate, or the Resident Commissioner from Puerto Rico.

(n) When the flag is used to cover a casket, it should be so placed that the union is at the head and over the left shoulder. The flag should not be lowered into the grave or allowed to touch the ground.

(o) When the flag is suspended across a corridor or lobby in a building with only one main entrance, it should be suspended vertically with the union of the flag to the observer's left upon entering. If the building has more than one main entrance, the flag should be suspended vertically near the center of the corridor or lobby with the union to the north, when entrances are to the east and west or to the east when entrances are to the north and south. If there are entrances in more than two directions, the union should be to the east.

Highlighting One Flag At A Time

With 50 states in the US and 200 countries in the world, there are endless opportunities for you to highlight individual flags representing your employment base, membership, or community. You can also create an internal campaign celebrating a different flag each week, month, or quarter.

Have different people within your organization research the history of a particular flag and perhaps present a brief report during an upcoming staff meeting, chapter meeting, or quarterly review.

Your organization can also use this opportunity to have designated members or staff to talk about what their nation's flag means to them and any personal stories that are linked to the symbolic nature of the flag.

Online Flag Stores

Here are two companies that have extensive inventories of flags from around the world:

www.arlingtonbanner.com

www.carrot-top.com

Chapter 4

Tip #3: Volunteer With A Culturally Diverse Nonprofit Organization

Some of the greatest multicultural lessons can be learned while volunteering with a worthy cause on the local, state, national, or international level. You provide your sweat equity (Habitat for Humanity) or your technical ability via mentoring or tutoring organizations in exchange for the valuable new relationships you will form as a direct result of your commitment to the cause. And the more outside your normal cultural base, the better. The more you look for an organization that targets people who are culturally and ethnically different than you, the richer the experience.

Here's an example. You're a White suburban professional who only glimpses at an urban area while riding on the commuter train to and from work everyday. You see the news stories about crime ridden streets and high unemployment in neighborhoods less than an hour away from your home. You want to get involved, to make a difference, but don't know how.

Your solution: Join the local branch of the NAACP based in that urban area. That's the **National Association for the Advancement of Colored People (www.naacp.org)** that has been the champion for the underserved since its beginnings in 1909. It is one of the oldest and most effective civil rights organizations in the United States, rich in history and long in fighting for justice and dignity for all people.

Membership in the NAACP is OPEN TO ALL PEOPLE, White, Black, Hispanic, or Asian. In fact the NAACP was started by a multicultural group of social activists determined to end the lynchings, other acts of violence and discrimination against Black people during the early days of the 20th century. Moorefield Storey, their first national president, was White. Another co-founder and longtime editor of the NAACP's publication, Crisis Magazine was Dr. W.E.B. DuBois, a Black scholar and intellectual. Other founders of the NAACP included Black social activist Ida B. Wells and Jewish activist Henry Moskowitz. In later years the NAACP Legal Defense Fund included such legal giants like the late Supreme Court Justice Thurgood Marshall, who has a personal relationship to my family (that I will save for a future book) and Massachusetts' first African American governor (whom I campaigned vigorously for) Deval Patrick.

The NAACP has always and always will be a multicultural organization focused on social justice for all "people of color."

So you, the White suburban profession could easily take out a membership in the hundreds of local branches around the United States and join for less than $50. You would now be alone, because local arms of the NAACP, like the Boston Branch, who are my clients, have White members who attend the meetings.

The work that the NAACP does is dizzying: i.e. voter registration drives, mentoring programs, prison advocacy. predatory and lending watchdogs, and challenging the political relevancy of the Tea Party. Like any organization, your views might not completely align with all of the ideologies of the NAACP. But the work that they do in such areas as voter registration, might warm your heart and pull you onboard.

There are millions of local, national, and international organizations to identify and determine which one is right for you. Here's a list of diverse associations that will begin your search for making your personal case for multiculturalism. These are national organizations based in the United States and in no way preclude the opportunity for you to identify the thousands of worthwhile local organizations that would value your service participation to their needs.

Clearing House For Association Leaders

ASAE (American Society for Association Executives
www.asaecenter.org

This is a good place to begin your search for the right organization to give your time and effort. ASAE represents a cross section of large and small nonprofit organizations and the leadership of those organizations that are mostly based in the US. Founded in 1920, ASAE now has more than 22,000 association CEOs, staff professionals, industry partners, and consultant members. Search on their website for a local or national organization that meet your needs.

Hispanic/Latino Organizations

League of United Latin American Citizens (LULAC))
www.lulac.org

Founded in 1929, LULAC is the largest and oldest Hispanic Organization in the United States. LULAC advances the economic condition, educational attainment, political influence, health and civil rights of Hispanic Americans through community-based programs operating at more than 900 LULAC councils nationwide. The organization involves and serves all Hispanic nationality groups.

National Council of LaRaza   www.nclr.org

The National Council of La Raza (NCLR)—the largest national Hispanic civil rights and advocacy organization in the United States—works to improve opportunities for Hispanic Americans. Through its network of nearly 300 affiliated community-based organizations, NCLR reaches millions of Hispanics each year in 41 states, Puerto Rico, and the District of Columbia. To achieve its mission, NCLR conducts applied research, policy analysis, and advocacy, providing a Latino perspective in five key areas—assets/investments, civil rights/immigration, education, employment and economic status, and health. In addition, it provides capacity-building assistance to its Affiliates who work at the state and local level to advance opportunities for individuals and families.

Founded in 1968, NCLR is a private, nonprofit, nonpartisan, tax-exempt organization headquartered in Washington, DC. NCLR serves all Hispanic subgroups in all regions of the country and has regional offices in Chicago, Los Angeles, New York, Phoenix, and San Antonio.

ALFPA   www.alpfa.org

ALPFA is the largest Latino association for business professionals and students with chapters nationwide and over 19,000 members. ALPFA is dedicated to enhancing opportunities for Latinos and building leadership and career skills. ALPFA is a non-profit entity registered with the Internal Revenue Service. Membership is open to anyone who shares our values, vision, and mission.

As an African American I recently attended a local women's conference sponsored by **ALFPA**, was invited to become a member and joined on the spot. About 20% of ALPFA members are non-Latinos.

Asian American Organizations

National Association of Asian American Professionals
www.naaap.org

The **National Association of Asian American Professionals** (NAAAP) is anon-profit organization that cultivates, supports, and promotes Asian American leaders. NAAAP offers professional development opportunities on the local and national level, engages its membership in community service, and organizes professional networking events. Through NAAAP, members work together to enhance leadership in their careers and communities.

As the largest and fastest growing Asian American professional organization in North America, NAAAP continues to provide its members with the tools and resources to further career advancements and empower Asian Americans to become great leaders and reliable employees. Founded in 1982, NAAAP has since expanded to more than 25 metropolitan cities in the United States and Canada. NAAAP members are affiliated with either a chapter or a venture. Ventures exist as chapter start-ups throughout North America.

Arab American Organization

American-Arab Anti Discrimination Committee
www.adc.org

The **American-Arab Anti-Discrimination Committee** (ADC) is a civil rights organization committed to defending the rights of people of Arab descent and promoting their rich cultural heritage. ADC, which is non-profit, non-sectarian and non-partisan, is the largest Arab-American grassroots civil rights organization in the United States. It was founded in 1980 by former United States Senator James Abourezk; has chapters nationwide, and members in all 50 States. With headquarters in Washington, DC, the organization operates offices in Boston, Dearborn, and New Jersey. ADC welcomes members of all faiths, backgrounds, and ethnicities.

ADC is at the forefront in addressing discrimination and bias against Arab-Americans wherever it is practiced. It acts as a national and local framework through which Arab-Americans can channel their efforts toward making an impact in the public arena and also advocating a more balanced US policy towards the Middle East. By participating in a wide range of activities, ADC has made great strides in correcting anti-Arab stereotypes, prejudice and fear. Consistent with its educational mission, ADC issues a bi-monthly newsletter; Issue Papers and Special Reports that study key issues of defamation and discrimination; community studies; and legal, media and educational guides. Additionally, **ADC is a proud and active organizational member of the Leadership Conference on Civil Rights (LCCR) and the only Arab-American organization that is a member.**

Native American/American Indian Organization

National Congress of American Indians   www.ncai.org

The National Congress of American Indians (NCAI) was founded in 1944 in response to termination and assimilation policies that the United States forced upon the tribal governments in contradiction of their treaty rights and status as sovereigns. NCAI stressed the need for unity and cooperation among tribal governments for the protection of their treaty and sovereign rights. Since 1944, the National Congress of American Indians has been working to inform the public and Congress on the governmental rights of American Indians and Alaska Natives.

Over a half a century later, our goals remain unchanged. NCAI has grown over the years from its modest beginnings of 100 people to include member tribes from throughout the United States. Now serving as the major national tribal government organization, NCAI is positioned to monitor federal policy and coordinated efforts to inform federal decisions that affect tribal government interests.

African American & Beyond

National Urban League   www.nul.org

The National Urban League is a historic civil rights organization dedicated to economic empowerment in order to elevate the standard of living in historically underserved urban communities. Founded in 1910 and headquartered in New York City, the National Urban League spearheads the efforts of its local affiliates through the development of programs, public policy research and advocacy. Today, there are more than 100 local affiliates in 36 states and the District of Columbia, providing direct services that impact and improve the lives of more than 2 million people nationwide.

Chapter 5

Tip #4: Deepen Your Diversity Training

Go Beyond Diversity 101

I call it "been there, done that diversity training." Others refer to it as "check off the box" training. It's where a company pulls out all stops, whips up a new budget, and the latest greatest diversity trainer helicopters into your organization for a day of training. Only to leave with half of your needs unmet.

Or has this happened to you? You have a diversity department, maybe a chief diversity officer with a part time staff member. Your diversity materials look fabulous, and your new promotional campaign contains the right spin on your commitment to diversity. But something is missing. Your senior executives may or may not buy into the initiative. Furthermore, there's not enough buy-in with the rank and file or throughout the middle ranks of the organization to expect a diversity department with only 1.5 personnel to provide the catalyst for the paradigm shift needed to change hearts and heads within your company.

This is why you really need to go beyond Diversity 101 and create a climate for deepened diversity training throughout your company.

Fully Integrated Diversity Training

It takes a fully integrated diversity training initiative that will provide sustainable learning throughout your organization.

I have seen so much in more than two decades of diversity work. I have seen strong, vibrant organizations bypass diversity, thinking that they "don't have a problem and don't need training." Those type of organizations look at diversity as punitive programs used as compliance fixers for something done wrong. On the contrary, I have seen smaller organizations with small budgets initiative diversity programs that are viable, valuable, and credible programs that are driven from the top down and bottom up.

Diversity Should Never Be Punitive

First of all, too many organizations use diversity training as a weapon of last resort. Something happens at a company and a lawsuit is filed. As part of the settlement, the court orders mandatory "sensitivity training," and everyone begrudgingly participates. The resentment is so thick you can cut it with a knife. So when the selected diversity trainer is brought on board, an additional amount of time is needed just to clear the air.

How do I know? I have been that trainer and defused that type of anger and resentment in the organization that hired me. I have had angry participants walk out of my training session because my workbooks didn't have the union logo and weren't printed in a union shop. (In that instance I had to remind the participants that as a native of Detroit, Michigan, my respect for unions was probably deeper than theirs.) I have had other sessions where the participants used fictitious names, refusing to give me their real names. And I have had training attendees so stuck on that fact that an African American female was conducting the session, they could not get beyond my Black face.

Those kind of sessions require extra work because the staff members resent being forced to attend the trainings. Don't get me wrong. I believe circumstances sometimes call for mandatory diversity training sessions and I understand the reasons why they are designed in that manner. It's the way that they are rolled out that will make the difference between a positive reception or an angry one. Sometimes you need a marketing campaign prior to the launch of the training program in order to get buy-in from those who can influence others in the organization.

Top Leadership Takes A Pass

A few years ago I enthusiastically set up a meeting with a CEO to discuss the opportunities for diversity in his organization. Although there had not been any negative diversity incidents to call into question, there was still a concern that most of the minority employees were cloistered in low wage jobs in the bottom of the corporate structure. Few people of color held senior level jobs. It meant that a strategic effort was needed to change the dynamics of the organization in order to build a better diverse pipeline to the top.

It took some time to get on the CEO's calendar. He was a very busy man. We knew each other because of other work I had done, so I was not a stranger to him. When the meeting took place, the CEO didn't hide his boredom. He looked at his watch a few times, discounted the recommendations I made, and brushed off the meeting just like flies are waved away at a picnic. I never forgot that meeting. It became a reality check that all CEOs don't value diversity. Ironically although effective as a leader, the same CEO was ultimately pushed out of the organization because of a personal matter indirectly related to diversity!

When the CEO cares little for diversity, it's difficult to incorporate the concept within the organization. What's sad is that I see far too many organizations with that same record.

Many diverse staff members in the middle and lower ranks of the organization, with only a handful if any people of color at the top. It's even worse with the amount of diversity on corporate boards. To lack diversity in governance is a key indicator that there might not be an internal mechanism to maintain diversity and inclusion within the organization itself.

Training Partnerships: Getting Buy In From Key Team Leaders

One of the best ways to ensure the effectiveness of a diversity training program is to identify key team leaders in your organization who will publicly endorse the campaign. These could be managers, supervisors, team leaders, lead employees, or staff members who influence others. When I design a program for a company I ask for a small committee that can work with me to design the diversity training program. I like to work with them upfront and at the beginning of the process, rather than bringing them in when everything has already been put in place.

The more a team leader gets involved up front, the more they are likely to "own" the project. The less involved they are, the more likely they are to criticize, berate, or not support the effort.

Some time ago when I worked with a large public agency I made sure that key employees were onboard when we designed the diversity program for one of their departments. The agency was represented by several unions, and it was very important to make sure the union shop stewards were comfortable with the diversity program. We held meetings to review our training goals and objectives, and actively sought out their advice and suggestions so that their contributions would be included.

When you are working with a union shop or with an organization with team leaders who monitor the relationships between management and non management employees, getting buy in is critical. The influence and power of these key individuals warrant building a relationship with them first and including them on your design committee before rolling out any diversity program or initiative. If there are any problems or if your design is not in alignment with their values, you could rage an uphill battle without their support.

Use The Word "INITIATIVE"

Sometimes I alternate between Diversity Training Program and Diversity Training Initiative. I have done so in this book. I prefer using the word "initiative" because it implies a longer term commitment to the cause.

Initiative in the dictionary is the introductory step to an action. I like using the word because diversity's ultimate goal is changing behavior, and that takes time. We are asking participants to open their minds and follow our lead. You should find every opportunity to include diversity in their thinking, their judgement, and their actions. Those are tall orders and require a bigger word than merely one "program."

Steps For Impactful Diversity Training Initiatives

1. Make sure you get buy in from key team leaders.

2. Move beyond simple powerpoint slides when training.

3. Develop a multimedia strategy:

   --enhanced powerpoint slides

   --video clips

   --Audio clips

   --testimonials from key team leaders and internal/ external influencers

   --games, prizes, and team based exercises

4. Avoid information overload. Don't build in too much in one session.

5. If possible spread out to include multiple sessions.

6. Build humor and fun into your segments so it doesn't seem punitive.

7. Include exercises into your segments, even if it's a keynote.

8. Validate the importance of each attendee, even the disruptive negative ones.

9. Give homework assignments, even if the diversity training initiative is a one day event.

10. Award Certificates of Completion to everyone who completes the training.

Chapter 6

Tip #5 Knowledge Transfer: - Pass It On

The wisdom of my late parents barely grazed me in my teens, danced in my head in my 20s and 30s, and has now become locked in place in my fifties. What was dismissible years ago causes me moments of reflection (and terror) as the years go by and new generations unfold.

What is so stunning for me is realizing that the playmates of my adult children are now managing the workplace. The very youngsters who were in school plays or in my carpool are leading organizations, managing hundreds of employees and making strategic decisions that impact whole communities. It's taken a gradual shift in my thinking to move me from seeing them in the sandbox to now negotiating with them in business conference rooms, and the process is far from over.

The game is new and exciting and the rules have changed. Technology, once vast machines in cold storage rooms at MIT has become a daily Tweet, a LinkedIn connection or a text message meant for an entire office to read. Game On, and the question is, are you ready to embrace the generations who are already the emerging leaders of today?

Generational similarities and differences make our interactions so unpredictable. If you're a Baby Boomer unfamiliar with the sounds of Lady Gaga or Beyonce, how can you possibly build credible relationships with those twenty years your junior? And if you're a Millennial staffer scratching your head when the conversation shifts to Walter Cronkite's reporting on the Kennedy assassination, think again. It's time for an intergenerational tune up where cross talk and two way dialogue are the only way to move forward.

I realized several years ago that our society had failed to establish a simple and easy to use knowledge transfer system where one generation of workers could share the good, the bad and the ugly with younger workers. Mentoring is part of that process, but I am speaking of a technique that can be standardized and used throughout an organization or company. This technique could be a valuable resource as older employees nearing retirement are asked to share their skills, give insight and/or wisdom to younger staff members.

In planning for shared information between generations, you can even assemble a "Knowledge Transfer" tool kit consisting of the following components:

1. An **archive center** in your organization - **brick and mortar or virtual.** It can be either a physical room that is part of your library collection or a password protected website. The archive center would archive the approved senior employee interview recordings, writings, and other materials found useful such as books, magazines, or assessment instruments. Employees would be encouraged to visit the room/website often as they build on their relationships within your organization.

2. **List of 25 questions** to ask the senior employee

   Questions could include the following:

   a. What has been the greatest lesson you have learned since joining XXX?

   b. How long did it take you to feel confident about your skills before you started demonstrating your abilities to others?

c. Where has XXX excelled in global diversity? Where can they improve???

d. What person, department or manager helped you the most here at XXX?

e. Is there one idea, suggestion, or recommendation you offered that was appreciated and implemented here at XXX? What was it? How was it used?

(Remember to edit each interview before releasing them to your archive center/website.)

3. **Create a one page document** called "Lessons Learned While Working At XXX." This document could then be used for reference as your senior employee personalizes their own Lessons Learned document for your archives.

4. **Video record an interview** highlighting the career achievements of the senior employee. This is where they have an opportunity of showcasing the projects, relationships and achievements of their tenure with your organization. The video clip could capture one special story or several of them. Keep it total length under five minutes. Use a flip camera, camcorder or professional recording equipment to capture their thoughts.

5. **Give a small thank you gift** to show your appreciation for the senior employee taking time to complete the assignment. Years ago, retiring employees received a gold watch, symbolizing the years of services with a company. In the age of technology, why not give that special person a digital camera, iPad, Android Tablet, or other electrical device that symbolizes 21st century innovation?

Archive Center Annual Observance

In recognition of your mature employees, try producing an annual **Senior Employees Recognition Event** to debut your new archive center/website. Paying tribute to these "new inductees" is an excellent way to say thank you to long serving staff members whose contribution to the organization will be archived for generations to come.

The greatest way to show your appreciation to senior employees to recognize them at a public program organized by your company. Most people respond favorably to recognition that pays tribute to their strengths and talents on the job. Of course there are those who prefer privacy and shun the spotlight; however, most people embrace a public acknowledgment for years of good service. Your employees are no different and will leave your workplace knowing that someone cared about their service to your organization.

Capturing The Essence To Knowledge Transfer

With the rise of Baby Boomers leaving the workplace, now is the time for you to develop a systematic approach to knowledge transfer.   Design a program that you can replicate throughout your organization that builds an effective bridge between older employees transitioning into retirement and your younger employees who can use the knowledge for their own enhancement and productivity.

Chapter 7

Tip #6 Become A Better Storyteller

When you boil down the value of great journalism, you get a great story. A star reporter who stays on the story, expands its potential, checks the facts and documents its every detail in a compelling manner can emerge as a Pulitzer prize winning journalist. All from one story. Photojournalists like Steve McCurry of National Geographic captured the hearts of war weary Americans with one picture of Sharbut Gula, the be-witching 12 year old Afghan girl with the green eyes.

Words can tell compelling stories.

Photos can tell compelling stories.

Stories can teach even the most difficult and "anti-diversity" employee.

StoryCorps For The Workplace

To take your employees' accounts of worklife and the experiences they have brought to your organization, create Story-Corps for the workplace. According to their website (www.storycorps.org):

StoryCorps is an independent nonprofit whose mission is to provide Americans of all backgrounds and beliefs with the opportunity to record, share, and preserve the stories of our lives. Since 2003, StoryCorps has collected and archived more than 40,000 interviews from nearly 80,000 participants. Each conversation is recorded on a free CD to share, and is preserved at the American Folklife Center at the Library of Congress. StoryCorps is one of the largest oral his-

tory projects of its kind, and millions listen to our weekly broadcasts on NPR's Morning Edition.

There are extensive resources on the StoryCorps website that can be reviewed as your organization considers ways to create a bank of stories from your company. You can capture the "teachable moments" of older employees packaged in an approved template that can be used throughout your organization. The beauty of StoryCorps is the simplicity and elegance of the stories using a familiar easily recognizable format that captures the essence of the experience.

Creating A StoryCorps Template For Your Organization

You can fashion a template the same way that is done with StoryCorps' samples. One example could involve Jane Doe, your senior division manager who is nearing retirement after 25 years on the job. She can illustrate the way she took a difficult project led by disagreeable team members and completed the project on time and under budget. And Jane Doe can emphasize how none of her male colleagues believed that she had the talent or resilience to complete the project.

Teachable moments make great stories. And chances are if you don't capture them on tape, you will have experienced employees who will take their stories right out of the company with them when they retire. In capturing the stories, you don't want to make your senior employees uncomfortable by "sharing their secrets." Your objective is to help senior employees to share workplace routines, decisions and techniques that will help younger employees coming behind them.

Chapter 8

Tip #7: Create A Vision: The Path To Following Your Dreams For Diversity & Multiculturalism

What is vision? It's defined as an unusual discernment or foresight. Vision can also be characterized as the power to see what is NOT evident to the average mind. When you embrace multiculturalism, empowerment and diversity you're allowed to reach beyond yourself while setting a new direction that requires you to stretch.

How far can you stretch on your job, at home, or in your community? Can you put aside your past troubles and look forward to a brand new horizon of opportunities? Can you see yourself in a leadership role or accumulating wealth? Can you see the doors of protection and prosperity opening wide for your children or grandchildren? Can you see yourself becoming the vehicle of change for those who can learn from your misfortunes?

A personal vision will take you places never before imagined. See it, believe it, and know that your abilities and your vision will help your dreams come true.

Create Your Own Vision Statement

I belong to a wonderful congregation that sets aside the month of January each year to concentrate on creating a vision for the New Year. During this month our pastors, Rev. Drs. Ray and Gloria White Hammond deliver a series of electrifying sermons that articulates the vision each member of Bethel African Methodist Episcopal Church should consider. We are an ethnically diverse congregation, yet our shared values bind us together in a unified fashion.

I look forward to our annual "Vision Month," and take it upon myself to carry that concept into my personal life. In January 1998 I created my own vision statement that applies to my life today. It states,

"Carole Copeland Thomas will capture the essence of the human spirit by delivering messages of hope, interconnection purpose, courage, and faith to people throughout the world."

Each year from this one vision statement, I create a multipage document of targeted goals that is broken down into financial, marketing, product development, personal, educational, family, and spiritual subcategories. Every goal in each subcategory links back to my vision statement.

Here are some tips on creating a vision statement for yourself:

1. Use broad, expandable language in your statement.
2. Don't use the present tense. Use verbs that will connect to your future. (*Rebecca will capture, Douglas will embrace, Michael will unfold, etc.*).
3. Mentally stretch when creating your statement. Don't lock yourself into thinking too small.
4. Find a quiet, peaceful location when you're creating your statement.
5. Write your vision on a large poster board and display it in your home or office as a constant reminder of where you are headed in life.

Creating a personal vision statement and companion goals will take some time to develop. Think about establishing a multi-year system for yourself so that you merely have to update your goals and vision statement instead of recreating them year after year.

Empowerment begins when you take charge of your life by creating these necessary tools that will keep you centered, balanced, and focused on your path to success.

Empower Yourself To Dream

Establishing a vision is only the beginning of your empowerment process. You are also given permission to dream. Through your visualization you create dreams that ultimately turn into tangible goals and objectives.

What is a dream? The dictionary definition states it clearly: "A dream is a train of thoughts or images passing through the mind in sleep." It further describes a dream as, "A visionary idea, anticipation or fancy… or anything having a dreamlike quality."

Our goals, aspirations, achievements, and accomplishments in life so often start off as dreams, images passing through our minds while we sleep. Each one of us has the capacity to dream and the ability to create dreams the size of Mt. Everest. Our visions transform those dreams into journeys that can take us from our present state of existence to the unbelievable destinations in our future.

The key to all of this is believing in your ability to make those dreams come true! Hold fast to your dreams and believe in your ability to reach the impossible.

Our Ancestors Were Dreamers

It's amazing how Black people of the past dreamed dreams and reached goals with practically nothing. For years my father's mother eked out a living as a Bel Air, Maryland domestic making five dollars a week. As a single parent, Carrie Copeland Brown (or Nanny Carrie as I knew her) raised two sons, saw my father, Wilson Copeland, graduate from college in 1941, remarried, and took her life savings to purchase a home. All as a five dollars a week maid.

So many African Americans can share that same story of transforming humble beginnings into a lifetime of sacrificial achievement. Look at the nickels, dimes and pennies raised to start most of the Historically Black Colleges and Universities (HBCU). Janitors, street sweepers, cooks, and maids dared to dream the impossible and paved the way for their children to someday capture the American dream.

So the next time you complain about not having a second pair of designer jeans, stop, count your blessings, and be thankful for the five dollars a week cooks, maids and janitors of your own cultural heritage whose sacrifices made it possible for you to achieve success.

Starting A Dream Box

Before you finish this book, I want you to start a "Dream Box." Use any box around your home, or buy a new one. This will be a special storage place for pictures, articles, words, wish lists, or miniature items that resemble a future purchase or goal. What will you put in your DREAM BOX? Will you load it with lofty unattainable items, or will you pack it with possibilities, plans, and future dates that will plant the seeds of your future?

When I started my new home dream box in 1995, I didn't censor my imagination. I loaded that box with pictures of 7000 square foot luxury homes to cozy bungalows nestled between the trees of familiar city streets. Your dream box should capture the breadth of your possibilities including all the opportunities that you can possibly achieve. Want to buy a new home? Want to send your kids to college? Want to have the financial freedom to care for your aging parents? Want to easily give money to that new community center that must be built? Start with your dream box.

It's all up to you and it all starts with you. Your dream box is waiting to be filled with your creativity, your possibilities, and the plans of your future.

From Dream to Reality

In 1995, I started my dream box and filled it with magazines, books, pictures, and articles on building a new home. I set a goal to become a homeowner in five years or less. I visited new construction sites, and trekked through Sunday open houses just to see what was on the real estate market. Achieving that gigantic goal of building a house was about as far-fetched as you can possibly image. I was recently divorced with three teenagers to feed. As a struggling small business owner my cash flow was in constant flux. My "new house" savings account totaled less than $100. And the college tuition bills for my oldest child were always right around the corner. As impossible as my dream of home ownership seemed, I never stopped dreaming about building a new home.

What seems unimaginable can turn into reality when your faith, your commitment to your career or business, and your determination to turn the corner in your life empowers you to achieve the impossible.

With the help of loving family members, countless prayers, focusing on my business, and that dream box, I built my new home in 2001. I was only one year off from my original goal deadline. It was a tremendous victory for me, a divorcee who had overcome obstacles in my path. The thrill of my life came when I watched my house being built. Those six months of construction magic were some of the most joyous I've had.

You too can start a dream box that can be filled with the aspirations and ambitions of your future. Fill that dream box to the brim and cash in on the possibilities that are waiting for you.

Empowerment does begin when you believe in yourself.

Your Dream Box May Open Pandora's Box

When you start a dream box don't expect your friends and family members to immediately understand what you are doing. In fact, expect them to sometimes become your chief critics. They mean no harm; they love you, and want to do whatever they can to protect you. But sometimes those closest to you don't have a clue about all of the possibilities just bursting inside of your spirit.

Sometimes when you're planning for your future or dreaming about what tomorrow will bring your way, you need to carefully share your plans with the right people. During the early stages of creating your dreams, you should only share your thoughts with the most supportive friends, colleagues, and family members. They may not understand why you are planning certain things, but will remain encouraging and supportive of your aspirations.

So step out on faith, carefully pick and choose your supporters, and dream about the excitement of your future.

Chapter 9

Tip #8 Mix It Up: Sit With Different People In Your Cafeteria, Your Next Luncheon, Your Next Dinner Function

Dr. Beverly Tatum authored a celebrated book some years ago: Why Are All The Black Kids Sitting Together In The Cafeteria? We used this book as a required reading resource when I team taught a diversity class at Bentley University to illustrate the natural tendencies of people to "stick to their own kind" in social settings related to human interaction.

We all participate in this activity. When faced with navigating an annual banquet or awards luncheon, we'll sit with people we know or work with. The larger the event or circumstance, the more we gravitate toward the familiar, the friends we know, the people who look just like us. It's especially true with daily lunch habits in corporate, government or educational cafeterias across the United States. People will sit with other people who share common qualities with them. Ethnic, gender, regional, or ranking levels top the ticket in how we self select our connection to others in public surroundings. And the stakes are higher when we're faced with greater numbers of people we do not know.

Ever represented your company by attending an annual fundraising banquet hosted by a nonprofit organization? One thousand people in the room and the seats are largely unassigned. Most of the people are African American. You are not. You walk in and start searching for people you might know. You settle for sitting with people who look like you. This is human connection in its purest form. It's not racist. It's not discriminatory. It's purely instinctual self selection at its most natural level.

Or we can reverse the setting. You're a person of color in a largely white organization. You're in the cafeteria and it's your first day on the job. Once you pass through the food line, pay your bill, you spot the people who look like you. It doesn't matter that you don't know anyone. You're just looking for safe ground to eat your lunch. And the South Asian engineers in the far corner of the room look like the perfect group to enjoy your meal with.

Acknowledge, Accept, and Expand AAE

One of the fundamental principles of multiculturalism and diversity is recognizing the personal bias behaviors within ourselves. Yes I said it! We ALL have bias. We are ALL prejudiced. As members of the human race, we all exhibit behavioral tendencies that allow us to gravitate toward people just like ourselves, especially in unfamiliar or public settings. That includes lunchrooms, cafeterias, banquets, conferences, social gatherings, and awards programs. There is NOTHING wrong with these normal tendencies. I am just asking that you:

--**Acknowledge** that YOU are biased and pre-judge people, just like every other human being.

--**Accept** that bias and prejudice exist internally and with every other person.

--**Expand** beyond your bias and prejudice by crossing cultural boundaries and connecting with people who are DIFFERENT from you.

That difference can target race, ethnicity, gender, sexual orientation, geographic regions, religion, economic status, political perspectives, or physical size. By acknowledging your internal bias and expanding your horizons and cross the cultural boundaries, you'll be surprised at how the world will open up for you.

Here are six examples of how and where you can cross those cultural boundaries all round you:

1. Select 5 diversely different people you want to meet in your organization and offer to sit with them in your company cafeteria AWAY from your normal friends and colleagues.

2. At your next convention or conference, make a point to take extra business cards and introduce yourself to at least 3-5 new diversely different people each day of the event.

3. Read an interesting or controversial article (such as "Why Affirmative Action Is No Longer Needed") and use your new found courage to discuss the article with diverse colleagues at a quiet and neutral setting.

4. Proactively build a new relationship with a diverse adversarial colleague who could benefit from your experience, training and background. Offer to buy lunch and arrange a meeting to "clear the air." Listen attentively and don't get too defensive if the feedback you receive makes you feel uncomfortable and testy. Just listen, learn, and agree to disagree.

5. Find out the birthday of a diverse colleague, offer to buy lunch, and ask that other co-workers join you for a special celebration.

6. Call up and invite the minority members of your organization to a special "Meet and Greet" networking event. Select a time that is convenient for these association members, serve light refreshments (or a heavier meal) and showcase your association benefits while you get to know each member beyond their face and a name badge.

There is something about food in a social setting that changes the mood and atmosphere of a job, a workroom or conference site. Your task is to leverage the communal experience of food to build a strong cultural bridge to diverse colleagues and staff members.

Beverly Tatum's popular book encourages the reader to initiate cross cultural conversations in school, on college campuses and beyond. My challenge to you is to expand beyond the walls of your secure and safe group of friends and colleagues by branching out to meet the wider world that greets you every day at work, in your association, and in your community. It's a small step, but a very important one in building relationships with those whose racial and cultural identity is different from yours. It's a small step that can lead to bigger opportunities to expand your diverse network right around you.

Chapter 10

Tip #9: Visit The United Nations

One of the best ways to explore global diversity is to visit the United Nations (UN) in New York City. It's absolutely FREE to enter the building and walk around the public spaces that make the complex so special. I have visited The United Nations several times, and always find the experience akin to a trip around the world.

Most of the countries of the world are represented at the UN, and just being in the building connects you with representation throughout the planet. Their website is: www.un.org.

What is the United Nations?

This is how the organization is defined on their website:

www.un.org:

The United Nations is an international organization founded in 1945 after the Second World War by 51 countries committed to maintaining international peace and security, developing friendly relations among nations and promoting social progress, better living standards and human rights.

Due to its unique international character, and the powers vested in its founding Charter, the Organization can take action on a wide range of issues, and provide a forum for its 193 Member States to express their views, through the General Assembly, the Security Council, the Economic and Social Council and other bodies and committees.

The UN has 4 main purposes:

- To keep peace throughout the world;
- To develop friendly relations among nations;
- To help nations work together to improve the lives of poor people, to conquer hunger, disease and illiteracy, and to encourage respect for each other's rights and freedoms;
- To be a centre for harmonizing the actions of nations to achieve these goals.

For those living in the Northeastern part of the United States, a trip to New York City should be fairly cost effective and can be coordinated on your day off or during a planned vacation day. For those living in New York City, you have no excuse! It's a bus, cab or subway ride away to get to 1st Avenue and 44th Street. The complex overlooks the East River in Manhattan, and is a majestic sight for foreign visitors and citizens alike. Admission is free, and the building includes a sizable bookstore, various topic-driven world exhibits, and a cafeteria. You can take a tour of the complex for a reasonable fee.

For those in other regions of the United States or those outside of the UN, plan to visit the facility at the appropriate time of year when you can enjoy the facility for two full days. Of course New York City provides you with scores of other sightseeing adventures; however, there is something very unique about exploring the very halls where nation building and peace keeping involves the gentle art of diplomacy and skilled negotiations.

Even if you don't travel that much for personal reasons, a trip to the UN can fulfill a lifelong need to travel to a destination of extreme relevance to this world. On occasion you can actually observe one of the Councils or the General Assembly in session, when voting between the member states (countries) takes place.

You will not get bored, whatever you do. You can merely sit in the oversize UN lobby and people watch as a major activity. There are always groups of school students who are visited for an educational project. Diplomats from 193 countries walk the corridors in search for peace keeping alternatives for their region of the world.

And the United Nations has some of the finest programs aimed at enhancing the development and protection of women and children, including their well known UNICEF program
(United Nations Children's Fund). UNICEF provided critical financial aid and supplies duing the devastating 2004 earthquake and tsunami that struck Indonesia and other Indian Ocean countries and killed over 230,000 people. During that terrible event I donated to UNICEF because I knew that the money contributed would largely get to the children who were affected by that terrible disaster.

For more information visit www.unicef.org.

Here's your United Nations gameplan to help expand your global diversity abilities:

Step One
Plan a 2-3 day trip to the United Nations in New York City. You don't have to spend a bundle to get there. And you can find reasonable accommodations in either New York or nearby New Jersey. Public transportation is plentiful, with public buses that will practically drop you off at the the door.

Accommodations for disabled visitors are also widely available in the building.

Step Two

Plan your visit in advance. Visit the website: (www.un.org) and familiarize yourself with how you will spend your time during your visit. Call ahead and order tickets for the tour of the building. Plan your visit when the General Assembly is in session if possible. Create a trip itinerary so that every moment will count for the money you are investing in the trip.

Step Three

Select a country of interest and see how it's connected to the UN. For example, Kenya is a favorite country of mine. I simply logged onto www.un.org, and clicked through to the home page written in English. Then I typed "Kenya" in the search box on the home page, which took me to a long list of activities and issues about Kenya that related to the United Nations. I could then build in prescribed activities that connect to Kenya while visiting the UN.

Step Four

Start a Blog about your trip. I find blogging during an actual trip is the most effective way to "take people with you" on your adventure trip. By blogging during the trip you can describe the building, the people, the issues, the exhibits, the artwork, and your personal feelings about visiting such an important facility. Of course you should decide if it's appropriate to blog during the trip or after you return home. Just don't wait too long afterward. You might forget key highlights of the trip. To start your own FREE blog, visit www.blogger.com or www.wordpress.com.

Step Five

Continue writing and speaking about your visit to the United Nations. Write a commentary about your experience and submit it to your local newspaper editorial department. Create a trip report and distribute it to your friends, colleagues and family members. Step Four and Five are so important because far too many people travel to important destinations and never take the time to share the experience with others...in writing. Definitely share photos and video clips to enhance your documentation. Plan to visit the United Nations in the future. Stay connected by visiting their website regularly and signing up to their website.

Chapter 11

Tip #10: Write An Article About YOU

People are fascinated with the miniscule details of the rich and famous. Every savory episode is reviewed, discussed and critiqued in books, online, on television, radio and on the big screen. Americans can't get enough of the biographical highlights of celebrities, entertainers, athletes, and the well known.

As an empowered multicultural advocate, I ask that you re-harness that energy and research your own life, your own family, your own career path.

Write an article about YOU.

You become the topic of interest as you build a timeline that can be archived for benefit of your family and friends. The purpose is not to create a new narcissistic profile that will elevate you to stardom and annoy your friends. The intent of the article is to create accurate documentation of your life, your ethnicity, your career path, your interests and why you made key decisions in your life.

Only YOU can write this article. Only YOU can set the record straight about who you are and the path you've taken to get to this point in your life.

Once written, the article can be shared with close family members, trusted friends, and most importantly archived electronically or printed out as a hard copy keepsake for future generations.

Article Length
Your goal is to write an article between five and ten pages. That may seem like an awfully long article, but once you start you will be surprised at how your memories take control of the journey.

Write In Story Form
Instead of starting with a chronological beginning, ("I was born in Dallas, Texas on September 1, 1971), start with a personal story. Stories are effective teaching tools used through the centuries to make a point, teach a lesson or illustrate the value or essence of a person, situation or event. Most importantly, stories make a point to the reader that otherwise might not understand the importance of what they are reading.

For example, here is how I would incorporate a personal story into my article:

The occasion had to be quite special for my mother, Gwendolyn Copeland, to pull me out of school in the early 1960s so I could enjoy a uniquely different cultural experience. My mother was an educator, a high school counselor and the chief champion of making sure that my older brother and I received cultural enrichment as often as possible. On this special day, I was taken out of school as a rare treat to go to a matinee performance of The Metropolitan Opera, on tour in Detroit. "I want to expose you to the world." My mother's famous words. And she demonstrated her love by exposing me to the world of opera. I don't remember the name of the opera, but I do believe that the great soprano Leontyne Price was the featured artist. As one of few African Americans to perform at The Met, my mother thought it important enough to take me out of school so I could witness great music and a great black artist all in one historic afternoon in my hometown.

A seed was planted that day, because years later in the 1970s I became a music major at Emory University. And as a young college coed, I would think back on the great African American musicians like Leontyne Price, who paved the way for so many musicians of color to follow.

That is a true story I don't think I have ever told in public. Yet, it illustrates the love a parent had for cultural arts and the way she exposed her young daughter to opera. It also makes a strong statement about civil rights trail blazers like Leontyne Price, whose powerful voice made her an international singing legend.   My story mentions historical dates that places the performance at the same time of the civil rights era in Detroit. It also describes my mother, an educator and disciplinarian, who made an exception to take me out of school so I could experience the opera.

List Your Stories
Your story could be completely different than mine. That is perfectly acceptable. The point is you have thousands of stories in your head just waiting to be told to others. Try making a list of 10 stories that can help to tell your life history. List your stories first on a sheet of paper. Then put a date next to each story. Don't worry about the order of the stories at first. Just make your list and date them. Then eliminate 3-5 stories that can be saved for another article. Place the remaining stories in order and begin writing out each one.

Outline Of Your Article
Here is an outline of how your article can be written. You will ultimately decide the direction of your article. The important thing to remember is to write clearly so that the reader can easily follow your life from beginning to the present day. Five stories are also included in this outline. This article can easily turn out to be 10-15 pages long.

-Birth, Family History, Early Childhood
-Parents, Siblings, Grandparents Extended Family Members
-Your Race and Ethnic Background
-Significant Childhood Personal Story
-Teen Years
-Significant Teenage Personal Story
-Post High School - College - Work
-Young Adult Experiences
-Family, Dating, Marriages(s), Children
-Significant Young Adult Personal Story
-Mature Adult and Age Issues
-Faith - Religion - Traditions - Values
-Career Path - Jobs - Training - Skill Building
-Significant Adult/Family/Career Story
-Other Highlights Impacting Your LIfe
-Closing Personal Story

Send Your Story To StoryCorps (See Chapter Seven)

Why not take your story to the next level and archive that special moment through Story Corps? StoryCorps' website is loaded with countless stories of diverse individuals from all walks of life who have shared their stories in perpetuity. Serious subjects, humorous events, and reflective historical moments have all been captured in StoryCorps. It's worth visiting their website to see how you can construct your stories for your own personal satisfaction, for your family archives, and for archiving through the StoryCorps website.

Capturing The Essence Of Your Article

You can control your life events by writing an article about yourself. It's an exercise that can start small with 10 pages and can grow into a full blown memoir in the months or years to come. Sit down and outline your article and fill it with stories of personal importance and relevance to your autobiography. The therapeutic value of this exercise can improve the very outlook you have on you life and the diversity in your family, community, and beyond. Take a leap, and go on and write that article about yourself!

Chapter 12

Tip #11: Visit Washington DC

Washington, DC, the capital of the United States, is open to anyone in America and the world. With more than 600 million residents, it is the political hub of the US, where judicial, legislative and executive leadership decisions make or break the productivity of the entire country.

According to www.washington.org and the 2010 US Census Bureau here are some interesting facts about Washington, DC:

Officially founded on July 16, 1790, Washington, DC is unique among American cities because it was established by the Constitution of the United States to serve as the nation's capital. From the beginning it has been embroiled in political maneuvering, sectional conflicts, issues of race, national identity, compromise and, of course, power.

George Washington, the first president and namesake of the city, chose the site and appointed three commissioners to help prepare for the arrival of the new government in 1800. In 1800 the federal government consisted of 131 employees. Pierre Charles L'Enfant designed the city as a bold new capital with sweeping boulevards and ceremonial spaces reminiscent of Paris of his native France.

Benjamin Banneker, a self-taught African-American mathematical genius, provided the astronomical calculations for surveying and laying out the city.

- **Population: 601,723**
- **47% male and 53% female**
- **Greater Washington has the best educated work force in the U.S. with 49% of DC residents holding a bachelor's degree or higher (compared to 28% of the general U.S. population) and 22% possessing a graduate or professional degree.**
- **DC's population is 51% Black/African-American (compared to 13% of U.S. population) and 9% Hispanic/Latino (compared to 16% of U.S. population).**
- **Median age: 33.8**
- **Average household size: 2.11 people per household**
- **Median household income: $58,526**

Washington, DC is not just for school children on a class field trip, or the residents of the city or international visitors. Washington, DC is for YOU and me. If you are an American reading this book, you should put Washington, DC on your "bucket list" before you die. It's the city where our federal laws are made, where our President leads the nation, where Congress resides, where the Supreme Court is housed, and where every federal agency is located.

Washington, DC is the political brain of the United States. (New York City is the economic engine of the US.) And since I believe that politics is a part of everything we do, it is important for Americans to taste, touch and feel that very city where our federal political structure operates.

Multiculturalism, diversity and inclusion are impacted by politics. The very course of action for these concepts are largely determined by the political atmosphere of our nation's capital.

Plan Your Trip To The Nation's Capital

Much like your trip to the United Nations (Tip #9), plan the time of year you want to visit Washington. Of course if you live in or around the nation's capital, you have a distinct advantage over the rest of the countr and the world.

Congress

The US Congress (House of Representatives and The US Senate) vacations in the summer and returns to their home districts between July and September. If you are planning to visit your congressman in Washington DC, don't plan a trip in the summer. Their staff members will be available to meet you, but your congressional representatives won't be there. You can always meet your congressional representative in your home district any time of year.

Visit www.house.gov or www.senate.gov for more information.

It costs nothing to visit the senate and house buildings in Washington, DC. Just walking the corridors is an amazing feeling and gives you a sense of the enormous power in Washington. (And the food in the various cafeterias is amazingly delicious and reasonably priced, too.)

The White House

The White House is a majestic white complex overlooking the Potomac River. Originally built by slaves starting in 1795, twelve American presidents owned slaves, and eight of them starting with George Washington owned slaves while in office. (Source: cnn.com) One of my personal heroes, President John Adams, was opposed to slavery and did not own any slaves.

Unless you have a special invitation, the chances of you personally meeting with the President of the United States in the

White House is slim. However, that should not stop you from arranging for a tour of the White House.

Here is information from www.whitehouse.gov, on how to schedule a White House tour:

Public tours of the White House are available. Requests must be submitted through one's Member of Congress. These self-guided tours are available from 7:30 a.m. to 11:00 a.m. Tuesday through Thursday, 7:30 a.m. to 12:00 p.m. Fridays, and 7:30 a.m. to 1:00 p.m. Saturdays (excluding federal holidays or unless otherwise noted). Tour hours will be extended when possible based on the official White House schedule. Tours are scheduled on a first come, first served basis. Requests can be submitted up to six months in advance and no less than 21 days in advance. You are encouraged to submit your request as early as possible as a limited number of spaces are available. All White House tours are free of charge. (Please note that White House tours may be subject to last minute cancellation.)

If you wish to visit the White House and are a citizen of a foreign country, please contact your embassy in Washington, DC for assistance in submitting a tour request.

Supreme Court

The last judicial word lies with the Supreme Court. They interpret and rule on laws and cases in dispute that have been litigated in lower courts of law. Another majestic white building, the Supreme Court is the home of America's nine highest judges in the land whose presidential appointments give them a job for life. (Technically there is the chief justice and eight associate justices.)

Famous Supreme Court cases including Brown v. Board of Education and Regents of the University of California v. Bakke have everything to do with diversity and multiculturalism. Familiarize yourself with the Supreme Court and you decide if justice has been established by the highest court in the land.

According to www.supremecourt.gov, here is information on visiting the Supreme Court building:

Although the Supreme Court does not offer guided walking tours, visitors are encouraged to tour the building on their own and take advantage of a variety of educational programs including Courtroom Lectures, a visitors' film, and court-related exhibitions.

The Courtroom is located on the First Floor. Court sessions are open to the public on a first-come, first-served basis. In addition to the Courtroom, portions of the First and Ground Floors are open to the public. Highlights include the John Marshall Statue, portraits and busts of Justices, and two self-supporting marble spiral staircases.

For complete details, visit the website at www.supremecourt.gov.

Federal Agencies

There are countless federal agencies to visit while in Washington from the US Department of Agriculture to the Department of Labor to US Treasury (which includes the IRS). Perhaps you have a particular interest in fair housing and want to know if your local real estate agency is fairly treating customers and clients with the same level of professional courtesy regardless of their race, religion, gender or ethnicity. Your answers can be found at the US Department of Housing and Urban Development (HUD). Although their website is extensive (www.hud.gov), visiting the building and discussing your concerns with a HUD staff member takes your advocacy to the next level.

To see a list of all of the federal agencies and to learn more about the US federal government, visit www.usa.gov.

Why Washington DC Matters To Me: Delta Days

I have made countless trips to Washington, for speaking engagements, conferences, meetings with congressional representatives and just for fun. The importance of the city crystalized for me when I began attending the national legislative conference for my sorority, Delta Sigma Theta Sorority, Inc. in 2004. Called **"Delta Days At The Nation's Capital,"** (DDNC); this four day event attended by over 1000 association members from around the United States is filled with general sessions, caucuses, congressional meet and greets, workshops and a pinnacle trip to Capital Hill. The conference is strictly focused on issues relating to communities of color, and is a stark departure from the stereotypical images of campus partying, nonstop step shows and scenes from Spike Lee's movie, School Daze. Delta Sigma Theta as a 501(c)3 organization cannot endorse candidates. However, it exercises its power to endorse issues that matter to African Americans and all people of color. Political issues matter to us, regardless of the political official's party affiliation.

I serve as the Tri-State Social Action Coordinator for Massachusetts, Rhode Island, and New Hampshire and enjoy the state and regional social action activities held each year that are patterned after DDNC.

Delta means much to me, and its rich history in public service has benefited women, men and children worldwide. My late mother, Gwendolyn Copeland, older daughter, Dr. Lorna Thomas Farquharson, sister in law, Deborah Copeland, and several cousins are Deltas. To learn more about the history of this nearly century old African American sorority, visit www.deltasigmatheta.org. and also visit The National Pan-Hellenic Council's website, www.nphchq.org, to learn more about the other nine African American sororities and fraternities steep in a history of public service.

To me, Washington, DC is the city of the people of the United States, a destination where diversity, multiculturalism and inclusion matter.

Washington, DC should be visited by all Americans at least once in a lifetime.

Chapter 13

Tip #12 Audio/Video Record Your Oldest Relative

It was a very special visit to their welcoming Bel Air, Maryland home. I had visited Bel Air since childhood, but this visit would be memorable. I sat before my only first cousin and his mother and the stories leaped out faster than you could blink an eye. I quickly turned on the portable cassette tape recorder and let the conversation begin.

Ironically this would become the last time I would have a kitchen table conversation with my first cousin, Rev. Charles Copeland and his widowed mother, my aunt, Mrs. Marguerite Copeland. Both died within a few short years of recording this conversation. After Charles died I gave a copy of the conversation to his wife and adult children, my cousins, Laura, Vanessa, Charles, Denise and Tawana. All had had a keepsake and a teaching tool to replay, reflect, and pass on to the next generation. The tapes were also available for friends and colleagues to learn more about the Copeland Family as they had migrated from South Carolina to Maryland.

At family reunions (learn more about them in the next chapter) I have videotaped cherished loved ones in their golden years whose stories anchored our genealogy tree. Their facial expressions, long pauses, and funny jokes all captured on tape. And even those family members who were reluctant to talk on camera, soon relaxed to the lure of a new family treasure chest of archived memories.

So I urge you, before you let more time escape, to capture the stories, memories, disappointments and triumphs of your oldest relatives on audio and video recordings. They will provide magical opportunities for you to preserve your history for your next generations to come.

Expensive Equipment NOT Needed

With this age of modern technology, you don't have to empty your savings account to buy fancy equipment to begin your recording project. Many of today's smart phones have decent cameras and video units to serve as your recording equipment. Or you can invest in less than $1000 and purchase a "prosumer" video or digital camera. Even the popular "flip cameras" now have HD capabilities and take very good footage.

I suggest that you shop around either in your local electronics store or online to find the best value for your dollar. Websites to consider when comparison shopping or learning ore about quality equipment include the following:

www.dpreview.com
www.photographyreview.com
www.digital-photography-school.com
www.videomaker.com
www.pricegrabber.com

Prepare Your Relatives In Advance

Older people don't usually like surprises. They like to know what's expected of them and how much effort is required of them to help support a project. If you're having a family reunion, meeting, wedding, bar mitzvah or even it it's a funeral, do what you can to prepare your relatives in advance that you are going to interview them on tape.

Create the questions and send them to your family members before the day of the event. Assure them that this will be an enjoyable experience, and let them know that you anticipate no surprises during the interview. The more relaxed they are, the better the interview outcome. If your relatives are nervous or not comfortable with being interviewed, try to conduct the session in their home before your family gathering, if you live close enough to each other. Or plan a special trip and visit special members of your family who are not able to travel because of poor health, caregiving requirements, or other personal circumstances.

Ask Good Questions

With your equipment in place and your special relatives waiting for their special moment, now you are ready to create your questions.

I encourage you to visit www.storycorps.org to learn more about how to create memorable interviews that will capture your relatives best stories. Diversity and multiculturalism embrace stories in the attempt to capture the cultural strengths of our racial and ethnic identifies. So the better your questions, the deeper level of understanding you will have for your family members.

Here are some questions to include in your interview. Select the appropriate ones and modify accordingly:

• Tell me about your birthplace. When were you born? Hold long did you live there?

• What about your parents? Where were they from? How did they meet?

• And your brothers and sisters? Are/were they younger or older? Were you a middle child?

• Was diversity a big factor in your household? How much diversity existed in your community/neighborhood when you were growing up?

• Your own spouse, children, grandchildren, nieces and nephews...Tell us who they are and what they mean in your life.

• What one event or situation has brought you the most happiness in your life?

• How have you overcome your greatest tragedy?

• If you could live your life all over again, what would you change?

• What advice can you pass on to the next generation?

• Did we leave anything out? Any additional stories to share?

What If You Are Adopted? Or Went Through Foster Care

This section of the book may be quite sensitive for those readers who are adopted or who grew up in foster care. Every situation is different. Some adoptive parents never hid the adoption process from their children. Others kept everything a secret. And those who have gone through foster care might find this section difficult because the foster care experience prevented any opportunity to properly connect with biological relatives and family members.

You will have to decide for yourself what make sense to attempt. The more direct communications you have with your adoptive/forster parents, the better the opportunity to reach out to biological family members.

I recommend two excellent memoirs and a very good movie on the subject of race, adoption and foster care may help you decide the path that's right for you:

A Chance In The World: An Orphan Boy, A Mysterious Past, And How He Found A Place Called Home
by Steve Pemberton (2012)

The Women Who Raised Me by Victoria Rowell (2008)

Movie: **Deep In My Heart** (1999)

Painful Past: What If You Don't Want To Dig Into Family Secrets?
Perhaps your family background is too painful to unearth. The sins of the past have been buried, and talking to that special family member will set off a series of uncomfortable triggers in the recess of your memory bank.

Simply skip this chapter for now, or forever. You decide how much information you want to archive and which stories are safe or clean enough to see the light of day. Select your relatives carefully and gently explain your perspective before beginning any interviews. If handled appropriately, unearthing the past might prove to be therapeutic for you and your family.

Post Production and Editing Your Recordings
Once you conduct your interviews, you will have a fair amount of unedited recordings for your new family history file. There are countless editing software programs. Audio programs for Macs include Garage Band and for PCs Audacity. Video programs include iMovie and Final Cut Pro for Macs and Adobe Premiere Elements for PCs.

Do a search online to find out tricks and techniques for editing your interviews. The most important thing to remember is to create short, interesting segments, no more than five minutes in length. Two to three minutes is actually ideal, will bring those listening or watching back for more.

Think about creating a family series of interviews with short segments that everyone will enjoy. You can even duplicate your recordings, create CDs and DVDs, and give them away to your relatives as gifts during the holiday season.

Set Up A YouTube Channel (See Chapter Eighteen)
The ultimate to your family history recording project is setting up your own YouTube Channel at www.youtube.com. It's absolutely free and gives you an opportunity to archive your new family recordings in one place online. There is a way that you can make your channel password protected and limited to a small number of family members, too. You decide if you want just a select few to explore your family history or a worldwide audience to enjoy your family's journey.

You can also create a PowerPoint slide version of your audio recordings and post them on your YouTube Channel. Again it's important to remember to keep your recordings short, no longer than five minutes long. The rich history of your family, your ethnicity, and the trials and triumphs of your relatives can tell the best diversity story ever. It's all how you prepare the questions, help your relatives to feel comfortable during the recording session, and provide crisply edited audio/video clips that will encourage others to watch your YouTube Channel.

In summary, here are seven steps to consider when recording your family members:

1. Buy affordable equipment.
2. Prepare your relatives for the interview.
3. Ask good questions.
4. Treat adoption circumstances carefully.
5. Think twice about interviews if it digs up a painful past.
6. Spend time editing your audio or video clips.
7. Upload your family recordings on your own YouTube Channel.

Chapter 14

Tip #13: Start Or Expand Your Family Reunion

The Gaines Family In The Shadows Of American History

The pieces started coming together more than 25 years ago when The Gaines Family of Columbus, Georgia began a new tradition of gathering every other summer to connect, reflect and pay tribute to a 200 year African American story. The Gaines Family members are the original descendants of 18th century William and Louisa Gaines, two slaves on a colonial Georgia plantation who fell in love and were allowed to marry. In fact during an era when slave families were routinely broken up and sold to other plantations, this couple was allowed to stay together and raise their 14 children.

One of their 14 children was Gus Gaines, who also had 14 children. From that lineage ultimately came Sarah Gaines Charleston, my maternal great grand mother. Her parents and her relatives ultimately owned 600 acres of sweet Georgia land shortly after the Civil War had ended. When the US Government came knocking on their door, asking to buy great grandmother Sarah's land by imminent domain at the turn of the 20th Century, her family patriotically sold their precious property so that the now famous military base, Fort Benning, could be built. Her family pocketed the money, moved to nearby Columbus, Georgia and began sending the children to college. As a result, my own children and my brother's daughter, Lauren Copeland Morgan, make up the fourth generation to attend and complete college.

Keeping The Family Connected Through The Gaines Family Reunion

That is a slice of my family story. It gets played out at each family reunion, along with the scores of other stories of the Gaines Family members who travel from city to city every other year for the reunion. The family reunion came to Boston for the first time in 2012 with my daughter, Michelle Thomas, serving as the local host. The reunion has also been hosted in Atlanta, Baltimore, Detroit, Chicago and our original home, Columbus, Georgia. It's a four day weekend celebration of fun and reconnections. Family historian, Clarence Gaines, has meticulously traced our family history back to William and Louisa Gaines, traveling the country and visiting courthouses and archive centers in his ongoing research project. Cousins Lula McKeever and Theresa Johnson are two of our eldest leaders, who lovingly keep the family events moving forward from year to year. Cousin Keith Williams follows their lead by overseeing family activities with administrative professionalism. And other family members, including Anne Lansey, Nikki Law, Mercedes Harris, Benjamin Caulton, and so many others keep the spirit of family traditions alive and well.

Connecting The Family Throughout The Year

We now have a private family Facebook page so that we can stay connected to each other. A quarterly newsletter highlights family achievements, graduations, marriages, and tributes to those who have died. We even have the entire family divided into regions, with the Family Reunion weekend traveling to alternative regions every other year.

My Family Reunion Story Can Inspire Your Own Quest For Diversity

The importance of me retelling my own story is not to showcase my bragging rights. It's to demonstrate that despite the tragedy of slavery, African Americans CAN trace their roots for several generations and create a multiyear celebration steeped in tradition and heritage. And like many families, the Gaines are multicultural with White, Asian and Hispanic family members. My own son in law, Jerome Farquharson, was born and raised in Jamaica. There were slave owners in my family who raised two sets of children with White wives and slave "wives" during the same time period. (That is why I...and many other African Americans....have light skin.)

My brother, Wilson Copeland II, is a well respected lawyer in Detroit. He follows in the rich tradition of our cousin Donald Gaines Murray, who was denied entry into the University of Maryland Law School in the 1930s. Denial didn't stop the dreams of Donald Gaines. He was represented by family friend Thurgood Marshall and Charles Hamilton Houston who ultimately won a court case against the university; thus ushering in Donald Gaines Murray as the first African American to enter the law school. Thurgood Marshall went on to become the first African American Supreme Court justice of the United States.

Start Small Then Build The Event
If you are new to family reunions, it's best to start small. Send out an electronic notice to round up your relatives and plan an evening to get together. Nothing fancy. Just dinner at the home of one family member or select a favorite restaurant at a convenient location and bring the family together for a few hours of socializing, collecting important dates, and swapping stories. Make sure one person is in charge of organizing the evening and handling all of the logistics. Another family members can serve as the evening's emcee, and another can perform or entertain. Like many single events, planning is the key to the success of the evening. And the right kind of small event can lead to bigger ones in the years to come.

Build On A Strong Event Platform

It's quite alright to keep your family reunion event small for several years. Perhaps an evening gathering once every other year is sufficient. Remember you can always supplement your face to face meeting with a social media presence (Facebook), conference calls and newsletters (electronic or print).

When your family is ready expand your annual or biannual gathering to a full day event or a weekend reunion. Similar to the Gaines Family, here is a suggested weekend reunion that can be held at a designated hotel:

Thursday Evening: Arrival to the hotel, Registration, Family Opening Reception

Friday: City Tour to historical sites or social family locations
The 2012 Gaines Family visited African American historical sites in Boston thanks to the tour operators at www.discoverroxbury.org.

Afternoon Picnic at a nearby park
A favorite Gaines Family event

Late Afternoon Workshop or Meeting
Free Evening

Saturday   Morning: Workshop or Meeting Part Two
12 Noon to 5pm: Family Awards Luncheon w/Family Group Photo
Free Evening

Sunday	Several Options: Closing Family Brunch in the hotel Early Breakfast followed by Faith Based Service either in the hotel or at a designated faith based center. Close and Departure

Note: Sunday can be reversed or modified if the family's worship tradition falls on Saturday instead of Sunday. If the faith calls for a Friday Sundown tradition, that, too can be added to the schedule.

Family Reunion and Multicultural Implications

Diversity, Inclusion and Multiculturalism ultimately probe family structures, communities and personal cultural connections. One of the best places to discover the value of multiculturalism is in your own family, your own community, your own "tribe." Family stories make up the building blocks of the family network, and identifying, archiving and sharing these stories through the family reunion process will bring you closer to the people in your "tribe." Make it a goal to share your family experience with others who are different from you to help them understand your family background as you begin to understand theirs.

Chapter 15

Tip #14: Plan A Cultural or Religious Field Trip

Why Should Visit A Nearby Mosque or Cultural Center If You Are Not Muslim?

I'm now a regular at the **Islamic Society of Boston Cultural Center (ISBCC)**. I have attended public forums there, taken Sudanese women attending a peace conference to ISBCC and witnessed their prayer service on Friday night. It's a very festive and welcoming center, with Muslims and their families from the around the world who regularly worship there and participate with community activities.

Yet my favorite reason for going the ISBCC is to purchase the lovely perfume oil imported from Jordan and sold at their gift shop. Would be hard to find elsewhere, and the variety of oils and other items at the shop make it an enticing place to visit again and again.

The Islamic Society of Boston Cultural Center is open to ANYONE, and the community is always welcome. Here is section of the website explaining ISBCC:

A cultural landmark. The ISBCC is the largest Islamic center in New England, and the second largest on the East Coast. The 70,000 square foot building stands tall on Malcolm X Boulevard in the heart of Boston, a Muslim handprint on the city skyline.

The cornerstone of the New England Muslim community. The ISBCC is not just a mosque, but is also planned to house a school (by 2013), a library, an interfaith center, an exhibi-

tion space and a morgue. Every Muslim neighborhood in the greater Boston area has had a hand in its construction, and its leadership reflects the full diversity of our community.

Source: www.isbcc.org

Curiosity Should Feed Your Diversity Appetite

Why do I visit ISBCC? Because I am not a Muslim, but an open minded committed Protestant diversity professional who is always looking to learn. I have visited other mosques and hope to visit mosques in the Middle East some day. I have also visited Jewish synagogues, gone to Bar Mitzvah celebrations, attended Holi, the Festival of Colors at a Hindi temple, visited a large mega African church in Naiorbi, Kenya, and participated in a Haitian wedding spoken in Creole.

In order to understand other people, you have to see where they worship, how they marry, how they bury their dead and how they socialize with their "tribe." And the best way to embrace a real cultural experience is to get out there and participate in the experience first hand.

So, I urge you to plan on a future cultural or religious field trip right in your own backyard.

Benefits Of A Cultural Field Trip

I was an adjunct faculty member at Bentley University for ten years. While there, I enjoyed a multi-semester team teaching arrangement with other Bentley University colleagues. One of our primary class assignments was to send our students on an individual cultural field trip. Dr. Earl Avery, Dr. Duncan Spelman, Dr. Marcy Crary, Dr. Aaron Nurick, Rosa Hunter and Maurice Wright and I team taught together during different semesters, and enjoyed the rich exchange of ideas and unending exploration of our international student population. We challenged them to stretch beyond their comfort zone by planning a cultural visit that was ethnically and/or diversely different from their normal "tribe." It was always a highlight of our semester, especially for those students who really took the assignment to heart, stretched and were amazed by their experience. For some, it provided a permission slip to step outside of the walls of conformity and learn about other people. For others it was an uncomfortable experience dredging up old fears and stereotypes stored in the recesses of their minds since childhood. Despite the fear of unknown outcomes, it proved to be one of the most potent ways to teach diversity from a practical point of view.

Ten Ideas on Creating a Cultural Diversity Field Trip

Here are 10 different ways that you can expand your diversity knowledge base by exploring the cultural opportunities in your own neighborhood, community or region.

Remember to select an event that is different from your own cultural or ethnic background. Yes, you can take a friend, family member or colleague with you for moral support, but see if you can participate in the experience by yourself.

1. **Visit an ethnically different faith based worship service.** For example, if you are Whiete and Catholic, find an African American Baptist church service. If you are Black/African American, visit a Jewish synagogue service on a Saturday. If you are Asian, visit a Hispanic Pentecostal worship service. If you are Hispanic/Latino, visit a Muslim mosque or a Hindu temple service.

2. **Accept a friend's invitation and go to their family wedding.** Find out as much as you can in advance so you will know how to dress, how long the festivity will last, and what

kind of gift is appropriate to give. Remember that the worship leader may officiate the ceremony in a language other than English.

3. **Attend a funeral of a colleague's relative.** This could be a colleague's parent, grandparent, or other extended family member. Again, this person should be different from your own cultural or ethnic background and a different religious group. Please be respectful of the family during their time of grief. If appropriate ask questions about the service beforehand.

4. **Visit a gay bar.** This was a favorite field trip of my straight students at Bentley University. Ask around and find a venue that is frequented by gay and lesbian patrons. Try to go alone to maximize the experience of the exercise.

5. **Attend a community meeting of a local or national nonprofit organization.** If you are White, go to the monthly meeting of the local branch of the NAACP (see Chapter 4). Again whatever your ethnicity, attend a meeting of an organization that is racially or culturally different from your own.

6. **Serve disadvantaged people during the holidays.** Find a diverse nonprofit organization that runs a soup kitchen, serves meals to the needy on Thanksgiving or Christmas and volunteer your services. For example, if you are Black, White, or Latino, find an Asian American nonprofit that serves meals to the needy in Chinatown in your region.

7. **Visit a school outside of your community.** If you live in a suburban neighborhood find an urban school to monitor for a day. Call the school in advance and ask to speak to the assistant principal. Explain that this is a diversity project and you would like to visit the school as part of your assignment.

Don't forget that this might be an opportunity for you to return to the school to volunteer your services (reading to students, helping out as a tutor, etc.)

8. **Attend a culturally specific ethnic fair.** These are quite popular during summer months when warm weather mixes with food, music, dancing, entertainment and crafts. Be prepared to ask questions to festival officials about the importance of the event and why certain traditions are included in the festival.

9. **Attend a culturally specific film festival.** These events are gaining popularity around the United States and take place throughout the year. They feature a variety of short and feature length films on a variety of topics. The interesting piece is that many of the films are created by independent filmmakers, from teenagers to mature adults. For example in Boston there is the annual Roxbury Film Festival (www.roxburyfilm festival.org) held each summer over a four day period. Roxbury is located in a heavily Black and Latino part of urban Boston, yet its historical roots are deeply connected to the American Revolution. The film festival features films by young Black, African, and Latino filmmakers who often create their masterpieces on a shoestring. The end results are often amazing works of art.

10. **Volunteer at a senior citizen home outside of your community.**
They are precious members of our society, and senior citizens throughout our communities look forward to visits from friends, families and people like YOU. Select a culturally and/or ethnically different neighborhood and visit a nursing home, assisted living facility or senior citizens home. Call ahead and find out the visiting hours and guidelines for your visit. Perhaps you can speak to a group of seniors in their community room. Or maybe you can have lunch with one

special senior and share your life story with them whatever the circumstance, your visit will be warmly received by those who meet you.

Chapter 16

Tip #15: Expand Your International Relationships & Embrace Technology As An Integral Part of Your Diversity Gameplan

Using technology in your daily business activities twenty years ago would have been optional. You could have simply used the telephone, a fax machine and a postage stamp to run a diversity and multicultural business. Yes, there were computers, but many organizations operated with only pen, paper, typewriters, adding machines and endless face to face meetings.

I started my own business in 1987, in a small shared office in suburban Boston. I owned one Macintosh computer and purchased the normal paper supplies from my local office supply store. The computer was a side note, not necessarily essential to running my office. Now I can't run my business without my Mac computer. Upgraded of course to a laptop, my computer is vital to running my affairs. I have also learned how to work virtually, and can run my operations from my automobile, on an airplane, train, or at my dining room table.

I also have been a radio talk show host since the late 1990s. I used to drive to the radio station put my headphones on in the sound proof studio filled with audio mixers, reel to reel tape machines and a control monitor and wait for a signal from my engineer to start my show.

Now my radio program is hosted on an internet platform

(www.blogtalkradio.com/globalcarole), by simply using my laptop computer and my cellphone. I can literally broadcast anywhere in the world, as long as I have an internet signal. And I have done just that; I have broadcast my show, "Focus On Empowerment," across from the United Nations and on the convention floor of the National Black MBA Association National Conference in Los Angeles, California.

In my world, you simply can't operate a speaking, training and consulting practice without a serious investment in technology. The same is true for most businesses, nonprofits, educational institutions and government agencies in the United States and abroad. Even small pushcart businesses in developing countries rely on smartphones and other devices to bring in revenues by servicing their customers.

Using Technology To Build Your Diversity Advocacy Skills

My zeal for technology does not mean that you must learn and master everything in the technology universe. That's not necessary and is also probably not possible. My advice to you is to learn as much as you can about technology so that you can make yourself available to serve others and to help people because of your tech related skill sets.

For example, if you only use your computer at work for the essentials and you're serious about connecting with people all over the world, perhaps you should invest in a computer, smartphone and/or tablet computer for personal use at home. Today it's not a good idea to use your computer on your job for personal business anyway. In some organizations, that could get you fired. Digital equipment today costs a fraction of its cost five years ago, so start saving now until you can purchase new equipment. (I emphasize new equipment because technology changes so quickly you don't want to get saddled down with aging and obsolete devices.)

Set A Goal And Set Your Parameters

1. Decide upfront the purpose of using and increasing your technology skills. For example, perhaps you want to learn more about the people of India and a specific Native American community in the Southwestern part of the United States. You have a good working knowledge of your technological equipment and your ready to explore. Use one of the search engines like Google, Yahoo or Bing and insert key words in the search box to begin your exploration. Chances are you will find an organization in the region that lists their contact information (name, email address, phone number.). Click on their weblink and select information that pertains to your research. Definitely find contact names, email addresses and phone numbers of individuals related to the subject matter, especially those who represent nonprofit organizations.

Online Research Can Lead To Valuable International Relationships

You will be amazed at the new international relationships that you can begin with internet searches. Real people with amazing experiences. Here are three examples of how technology can expand your globally diverse network of new friends and colleagues.

Mahmud and Shahinoor Visram, Sun N' Sand Resort
Kenya In My Blood

In 2005 I traveled to Kenya for the first time with nine other African American women from Boston. We have since formed a nonprofit organization called the Kenya Sistahs (www.kenyasistahs.org). That life changing trip put me closer to the other side of the world and the continent of my ancestors like no other experience. My own father, Wilson Copeland, had lived and worked for the US State Department in Ghana, West Africa and Kenya, East Africa for 20 years, so the experience of vacationing in Kenya was a pilgrimage for me. During that first trip I savored every moment, ate delicious food, went on amazing safaris, and met warm and gracious Kenyans. I ended up befriending one of our tour guides, Naftal Kiambo Mwangi, and became his co-sponsor, allowing him to complete his high school education. Naftal is still my "Kenyan son," and I have enjoyed my relationship with him and his family for nearly seven years. He has worked through the years since high school and is currently pursing a college education in Kenya.

We returned to Kenya in 2007, and our group decided to host an international conference in Mombasa, Kenya, a beautiful city off the coast of the Indian Ocean. As a newly formed humanitarian organization, the Kenya Sistahs were focused on issues related to the women, children and families of Kenya. Months before the trip I started searching the Internet for sustainability groups, organizations supporting Kenyan women, and micro lending organizations. After weeks of research, I stumbled upon an intriguing United Nations article about a socially responsible resort hotel in Mombasa that financially support the neighboring primary school, provided drinking water for the community and bought local produce from community farmers. The author was the owner of the family run resort complex, and their philosophy was to live in harmony with the community, while employing and training as many local residents as possible. It seemed like an unbelievable organization, nearly 7500 miles from Boston. I was fascinated with every page I downloaded.

At the end of the article was the name and email address of the author/resort owner, Mr. Mahmud Visram. I took a chance, crafted an email to him expressing my interest in learning more about his socially responsible organization and clicked "send." I expected a reply, just hoped that Mahmud would know that an African American admired the community commitment his family had made.

About two weeks passed and I noticed an email from a Mahmud Visram titled, "Did You Receive My First Email?" I opened it and realized that he had actually replied days earlier with his original response. I checked my spam folder, and there was his original email. I read it with great delight, and realized that Mahmud was thrilled to receive my message. He gave me considerably more information about his philosophy, told me about his wife and children and suggested that we set up a convenient time to speak by phone.

We corresponded by email and arranged a time to talk. That was the beginning of my ongoing relationship with Mahmud and Shahinoor Visram, two of the most delightful and respected hoteliers on the planet. They are devout Muslims with roots in India, astute business owners who love their African heritage. And they are now my dear friends.

We ended up collaborating on our 2007 International Conference, and our group agreed to stay at their hotel while we were in Mombasa (we had stayed at a competing hotel during our 2005 trip). All of the details for the conference were made online! Our group received special sponsorship from the office supply store, Staples, that supplied us with over $1200 worth of school supplies. We packed every single item and other goods in our suit cases, and British Airways waived the extra baggage charges. While in Kenya we gave away all of the supplies to our partner organizations and worked closely with the Visrams and their staff members to finalize the conference.

The conference was a big success. Over 120 people from Kenya and Uganda attended our one day event at the Sun N' Sand Conference Center. The Visrams, who had agreed to split the expenses were so pleased with the turnout and outcome of the event decided on the spot to underwrite all of the food and beverage costs for group! We then took that money we would have spent on the conference and donated it to pay for the school fees of several young students at the Kikambala school supported by the Sun N' Sand.

It was a "win-win" for everyone. And it all came from an article downloaded from the United Nations website.

As Kenya Sistahs, we had operated on faith and good intentions. The Sun N' Sand, thousands of miles away had the same focus. We collaborated as a team focused on doing good for the community at large. Technology was the cultural bridge that linked an African American women's group to a Kenyan beach resort for a good purpose.

It's that type of true story that can happen to you if you fully engage technology in your diversity and multicultural journey.

Garth Dallas, Liverpool, England
Global Diversity in the United Kingdom

Nearly three years ago while working online, I received an email from a gentleman looking to verify if I was the person who was responsible for Global Diversity Awareness Month. It is a month long commemoration of diversity and inclusion that I started through Chases Calendar of Events more than 15 years ago (www.chases.com). He detailed that he was a diversity professional living in Liverpool, England and was reaching out to the originator of Global Diversity Awareness Month. I replied, verified that the month was indeed my idea, and arranged a date and time to speak with him by phone.

We did speak, and it was evident that he had done his homework. His name was Garth Dallas, originally from Jamaica, and a Liverpool resident for many years. Over the course of several months we explored our different approaches to diversity, the differences between diversity in the UK verses America, and opportunities to collaborate together through the commemorative month I had created. I learned a great deal about European diversity issues, including the importance of Liverpool as a historical center of Black heritage and that Black History Month was celebrated in October in the UK. (It is celebrated in February in the U.S.)

Through the years Garth and I have conducted international webinars, have responded to different diversity issues in our respective countries, and generally encouraged one another as our projects and workplace initiatives have progressed forward. All driven by technology, we have expanded what began as a simple email request to an international business relationship that benefits us in our respective countries.

Angela Bukenya
Google Diva and The Uganda Conference
It's happening with such regularity that I have grown to appreciate those who "find me" online. More than two years ago a vibrant young woman from Uganda "found me" and inquired about my speaking services on empowerment. She had done research on Google, learned that I had written a book (my first book titled Personal Empowerment: How To Turbo Charge Your Life Both On and Off Your Job) and was interested in hiring me as a keynote speaker.

The Ugandan organization of which she belonged, was hosting its first international conference in Boston, and she was the program chair. She was living in Spokane, Washington and using her technology skills to conduct her nonprofit work across the country and in Uganda. In the months following that initial agreement, we confirmed my speaking services for her upcoming conference, an I was introduced, online, to other members of the leadership team who were also planning the conference.

The conference was a success and provided me a golden opportunity to connect with the Ugandan community both in Massachusetts and beyond.   Since the conference Angela and I have remained friends, and I recently had the pleasure of attending her graduation from graduate school in Spokane.

All from a simple inquiry, my relationship with Angela is more proof that our world has grown very small because of emails, text messages, conference calls, webinars, website reviews and online searches.

You Need Technology To Build A Diversity Base
My charge for you is to begin or expand your comfort level and use of technology in the months and years ahead. Technology is here to stay, and anyone interested in multiculturalism, diversity and inclusion needs to have a good working knowledge of technology in order to build a credible network of friends, colleagues and advocates around the world.

Chapter 17

Tip #16: Social Media & Social Networking Part One: Using Facebook and Twitter in Your Diversity Activities

As of this writing, there are hundreds of social media channels designed to bring people together regardless of where they live and what they do for a living. Social networking web based platforms have literally changed the way we communicate and have altered the way news organizations gather and report local, state,national, and international news stories.

And social media is largely responsible for the dramatic shift in power in the Middle East. The Arab Spring revolutions from Tunisia, Egypt, Libya and ultimately Syria, social media has played a vital role in transforming tightly controlled dictatorship nations into democratically evolving countries.

It simply isn't in your best interest to ignore social media or social networking if you plan on fully engaging your multicultural plan of action. You need to understand their purposes and select how you want to develop your online game plan to advance your global diversity strategy.

According to www.socialmediatoday.com:
Social media is more akin to a communication channel. It's a format that delivers a message. Like television, radio or newspaper, social media isn't a location that you visit. Social media is simply a system that disseminates information to others.

With social networking, communication is two-way. Depending on the topic, subject matter or atmosphere, people congregate to join others with similar experiences and backgrounds. Conversations are at the core of social networking and through them relationships are developed.

Those involved in the Arab Spring revolutions used **social media** and that channel of distribution to tell people where to protest, who was safe to communicate with and what governmental policies were being challenged. In the United States, social media is now often used in civic activism to bring attention to a pressing civil rights story. The tragic 2012 case of the death of Trayvon Martin heavily relied on social media to bring attention to the untimely and racially motivated death. The young 17 year old unarmed Black teenager was shot and killed by an over zealous Floridian who falsely targeted Martin for criminal activities. Blog posts, online conversations, petitions posted on social networking websites and ultimately increased public awareness led to political changes, arrests, and criminal court trials in both the Arab Spring uprisings and the Trayvon Martin case.

Social networking uses specific websites to create, build and impact communities. According to Wikipedia:

A social networking service is an online service, platform, or site that focuses on facilitating the building of social networks or social relations among people who, for example, share interests, activities, backgrounds, or real-life connections. A social network service consists of a representation of each user (often a profile), his/her social links, and a variety of additional services. Most social network services are web-based and provide means for users to interact over the Internet, such as email and instant messaging. Online

community services are sometimes considered as a social network service, though in a broader sense, social network service usually means an individual-centered service whereas online community services are group-centered. Social networking sites allow users to share ideas, activities, events, and interests within their individual networks.

There are countless social networking platforms, and I encourage you to conduct an online search to find the platform that best serves your needs. You cannot use them all, so don't frustrate yourself by trying to understand the vast options available to you.

Carole's advice: Select no more than FOUR social networking platforms to use for your multicultural activities. This book focuses on the four platforms that Carole uses and represent the most popular ones in cyberspace. This chapter highlights Facebook and Twitter. The next chapter highlights LinkedIn and Youtube.

Facebook
www.facebook.com
Now the largest social newtworking websties on the planet with over 900 million users, Facebook is a worldwide community of users that started in 2004 allowing anyone 13 years or older to create a free online account.

Carole's Tip: Use Facebook To Create An Online Diverse Community Led By You
I have used Facebook for more than four years, thanks to the prodding of my daugher, Michelle. I have organically grown my list of more than 2000 "friends" to my Facebook page and decided from the beginning to allow people I knew and did not know to be added as "friends." I also created a group page for the Multicultural Symposium Series that has fewer "friends/members" than my original page. I welcome and

encourage people from different ethnic, political and religious perspectives to "friend" me, because it provides a richer more diverse conversation to occur when discussing controversial topics. Many of my "friends" live and work outside of the United States.

I suggest that you create or revise your Facebook page so that anyone can discuss current events with you. When discussing a topic, start the conversation and try not to censor the comments of your "friends" unless the conversation becomes violent, crude, or abusive. When US Senator Ted Kennedy died in 2009, I remember facilitating a spirited discussion with those who admired Kennedy and those who rejected him. Even though I am a Progressive Democrat and supported Senator Kennedy, it was important not to interrupt the flow of ideas and opinions on the right and the left at the time of his passing. It became an international conversation with several comments originated outside of the United States. During Senator Kennedy's funeral, I even reported live entries so that those outside of Boston could participate and reflect on the experience.

Here's a list of other ways to use your Facebook page:
- Survey your "friends."
- Announce an upcoming event.
- Talk about your favorite ethnic foods.
- Ask about where your "friends" were born.
- Post photos/photo albums of important events in your city/town.
- Write an opinion paper and upload it to your docs section.
- Post photos/photo albums of your family and tell your family story.
- Upload short video clips about your family or impor tant events.
- Send birthday greetings to your "friends."

- Start a controversial conversation (like same sex mar riage).
- As your "friends" to make suggestions about an im portant decision you must make.

Because your "friends" are not anonymous, they are proba- bly not going to send you lewd, vicious or crazy comments. That's the safety value that allows you to fully explore diver- sity, with your "friends" as your audience.

The informal nature of Facebook allows for personal explora- tion with other people in your neighborhood, your family, or half way around the world. Use it to explore a wider world outside of your traditional network while sharing selective information about yourself with others.

Twitter
www.twitter.com

Now one of the fastest growing social newtworking and microblogging websties on the planet with over 140 million users, Twitter is a worldwide community of users who send text based entries of 140 characters or less. Started in 2006 anyone of any age can create a free online account. Twitter is popular with celebrities, entertainers and political officials.

Twitter is also on the cutting edge of delivering breaking news stories before major news organizations make their announcements. The 140 character postings are appropriately called "tweets."

Carole's Tip: Use Twitter To Follow Breaking News Stories Around The World

I signed up to Twitter kicking and screaming in 2009, and felt that I already had a large enough footprint in the social networking arena. My friend, Rosemary Horner, insisted on giving me a tutorial late one night in early June so that I would stay ahead of the curve of my online strategy. I grudgingly agreed to set up a conference call with Rosemary, but really had no intention of taking Twitter seriously. What could you really say in 140 characters anyway?

My tutorial lasted almost two hours, and I happily signed off, and thanked my teacher for sharing her insight and knowledge with me. That next week I continued on with my business activities and checked my new Twitter account occasionally. I started "following" certain people and allowed others to "follow" me. Unlike Facebook, there is a degree of anonymity, and I learned how to block followers that were really porn sites.

My introduction to Twitter occurred one week prior to the June 12th presidential elections in Iran. Things seemed somewhat peaceful prior to the elections, but chaos erupted with declarations of widespread fraud shortly after the elections ended. That weekend marked my first full week on Twitter, and I kept noticing #iranelections under the Trending Topics section on my homepage. I clicked on the link and was introduced to an entire new world of social activists inside Iran desperately trying to tell the world that violent post election protects were erupting in Tehran and other parts of the country.

CNN on that Saturday was showing re-runs and not actively covering this fast breaking news story. The social activists pleaded with CNN, BBC and other news organizations to cover the story. People were getting arrested by the police, were getting beaten up and were dying inside of Iran, and the major media outlets were largely asleep at the switch. Only those active on Twitter and other social networking sites were covering the story live. Finally by Sunday night CNN, BBC and the others realized that Twitter and the other online platforms had scooped one of the biggest stories of the month. They quickly dispatched their top reporters to the region and joined in the coverage.

Since that one incident, Twitter has captured a commanding lead in covering late breaking news stories around the world. CNN, BBC and the others no longer take social networking or social media for granted.

I do tweet about 2-3 times per week, but largely use the platform to follow top news stories. I learned about the death of Osama bin Laden and Libya's Muammar Gaddafi first on Twitter before their assassinations were announced on the air.

Here's a list of eight other ways to use your Twitter account:
• Use a hashtag (the pound/number symbol #) to follow topics, events, and people.

•Create your own hashtag on a topic that interests you such as #diversityleaders.

•Follow topics including "diversity, #multicultural, and #inclusion.

•Identify and follow celebrities, journalists, and business professionals of interest.

•Create a hashtag with your next event or conference such as #asaenewyork2012.

•Follow those who follow you who share your interest in diversity.

•Visit websites that are linked to tweets you receive on key topics.

•Listen to recommended audio clips and watch video clips on key topics of interest.

Chapter 18

Tip #17: Social Networking & Video Sharing Websites
Part Two: Using LinkedIn and YouTube in
Your Diversity Activities

The two additional platforms that weigh heavily into my multicultural strategy are LinkedIn and YouTube. Again I encourage you to identify no more than four social networking sites to conduct your ongoing multicultural gameplan. These two websites are important players in the ever expanding global online community.

LinkedIn
www.linkedin.com
LinkedIn is a social networking website that targets a worldwide community of 161 million business professionals. According to their website here is pertinent information about LinkedIn:

- LinkedIn started out in the living room of co-founder Reid Hoffman in 2002.
- The site officially launched on May 5, 2003. At the end of the first month in operation, LinkedIn had a total of 4,500 members in the network.
- As of March 31, 2012 (the end of the first quarter), professionals are signing up to join LinkedIn at a rate of approximately two new members per second.
- The company is publicly held and has a diversified business model with revenues coming from hiring solutions, marketing solutions and premium subscriptions.

LinkedIn Facts
- As of March 31, 2012, LinkedIn operates the world's largest professional network on the Internet with 161 million members in over 200 countries and territories.
- Sixty-one percent of LinkedIn members are located outside of the United States, as of March 31, 2012.
- LinkedIn members did nearly 4.2 billion professionally-oriented searches on the platform in 2011 and are on pace to surpass 5.3 billion in 2012.
- Headquartered in Mountain View, Calif., LinkedIn also has U.S. offices in Chicago, Los Angeles, New York, Omaha and San Francisco. International LinkedIn offices are located in Amsterdam, Bangalore, Delhi, Dublin, Hong Kong, London, Madrid, Melbourne, Milan, Mumbai, Munich, Paris, Perth, São Paulo, Singapore, Stockholm, Sydney, Tokyo and Toronto.
- The company's management team is comprised of seasoned executives from companies like Yahoo!, Google, Microsoft, TiVo, PayPal and Electronic Arts. The CEO of LinkedIn is Jeff Weiner.
- LinkedIn is currently available in seventeen languages: English, Czech, Dutch, French, German, Indonesian, Italian, Japanese, Korean, Malay, Polish, Portuguese, Romanian, Russian, Spanish, Swedish and Turkish.
- As of March 31, 2012, LinkedIn has 2,447 full-time employees located around the world. LinkedIn started off 2012 with about 2,100 full-time employees worldwide, up from around 1,000 at the beginning of 2011 and about 500 at the beginning of 2010.

Like most of the other social networking websites, LinkedIn is free, even though they do have more advance options that can be purchased by each user. I have used the free version of LinkedIn since 2007 and find it an ever extremely useful tool for business exchange. I have organically grown more than 1200 "connections," and I am always looking for more ways to expand my business connections through their website.

LinkedIn works differently from Facebook or Twitter. There is a more formal process of accumulating "connections." You have to either know the individuals, connect with them through group/organization affiliations, or get introduced to them though your direct LinkedIn "connections." It's frowned upon to reach out to individuals you do not know. The formality of getting introduced is part of the LinkedIn process. Once a person confirms as your first line "connection," you are free to communicate with them by email or phone.

The **LinkedIn Groups** provide some of the most valuable ways to communicate on the website. There are more than one million groups, so your choices are endless! Many of the groups are open, while others are closed to selected individuals. I have found some very good groups focused on domestic and international diversity issues. Through the discussion groups you can contribute to the conversation while expanding the relationships in your professional network of friends and colleagues.

Here's a list of seven other ways to use your LinkedIn account:
•Decide in advance the type of "connections" you want to include in your LinkedIn portfolio. Consider the type of profession, position within an organization, etc. that interests you.
•Decide in advance your longterm goal(s) for using LinkedIn.
•Explore the large number of groups available and identify up to 50 that can address your diversity and multicultural game plan.

•Actively participate in the discussions generated through the LinkedIn Groups.

•Identify a finite number of "connections" who share your interest in diversity. Determine the most appropriate way to learn more from these individuals through an expanded relationships.

•Initiate a new question in one or more of your groups at least once per month.

•Consider starting a LinkedIn Group if there is not one specific to your diversity issues.

YouTube
www.youtube.com

YouTube is a free video sharing website that allows an average person to upload a video file and share it with viewers around the world. There are other video sharing webites on the Interet providing a wide range of options, however YouTube is by far the most popular site in cyberspace.

YouTube's website states the following:
Founded in February 2005, YouTube allows billions of people to discover, watch and share originally-created videos. YouTube provides a forum for people to connect, inform, and inspire others across the globe and acts as a distribution platform for original content creators and advertisers large and small.

In 2006 I had never heard of YouTube until I was speaking in El Salvador. Students from a prestigious university who were participating in our weekend leadership institute pulled up a video clip on YouTube and used it in their presentation. I was intrigued. I opened my laptop and accessed the Internet, using the wifi system the school provided. I typed in the site's URL and there was an intriguing website loaded with short video clips from around the world. There was every imaginable topic covered on the website, and anyone anywhere in the world could shoot a video and upload it onto YouTube in minutes.

Now six years later YouTube is a mainstream platform that has provided a springboard for budding artists to get "discovered." It also has sounded the death knoll for politicians who said and undertook inappropriate actions in front of an unforgiving camera. There are endless "how to" videos on YouTube, and countless ways to express diversity and multicultural ideas on camera.

I set up a free "YouTube Channel" some years ago and have uploaded a select number of video clips to the site. I have many more videos to upload and plan on expanding my use of the channel as the Multicultural Symposium Series continues to expand. YouTube videos can also become effective marketing vehicles, driving traffic to your website for more details on your products, services or organization.

Here's a list of eight other ways to use your free YouTube account:
• Officially register as a YouTube user to gain access to the wide variety of videos on the website.
• Consider starting your own YouTube Channel for your diversity related videos and projects.
• Explore other diversity-related videos and share your thoughts in the comment section.
• Create a series of diversity and multicultural videos that capture your thoughts on specific topics and issues.
• Start a YouTube Channel for your company, organization or group that can showcase the many ways you are addressing diversity and multicultural issues.
• Use YouTube videos for your training programs on the job.
• Use YouTube videos for on the job lunch and learn programs.
• Improve your presentations by using YouTube videos in your presentations (give full credit when citing the source of the video).

BONUS TECH RESOURCES TO CONSIDER
SKYPE
www.skype.com
Talk to your new friends and colleagues around the world by using a unique software product called SKYPE. It's a free voice-over-Internet Protocol (VOIP) service that you download onto your computer, allowing you to make free phone calls to anyone in the world who also has SKYPE on their

computer. You can also use SKPYE to make calls to non-SKYPE users, however, there is a charge for that service.

After connecting with my British colleague, Garth Dallas, we regularly met online using SKYPE. There is no time limit, and you can talk to your friends, family members or colleagues for hours. All you need is your computer, laptop, a headset and a microphone.

Conference Calling
www.freeconferencecalling.com

Teleconferencing involves free bridge lines allowing you to conduct a meeting by telephone or a workshop from 2 to thousands of people. Your call can be recorded and down-loaded as a MP3 file afterward.

My travel to and from meetings has been reduced by more than 50% since using this free conference call service for more than ten years. Previous bridge lines did have a charge, but the current services do not. They make a percentage of revenue on the actual phone call to the desig-nated number that you make when you join or host the call.

I have been a part of domestic and international conference calls for years and find that they provide a useful and cost effective way to communicate with others regardless of geo-graphical locations. I started my distant learning workshops (teleseminars) using conference calls way back in 2001.

Webinars
www.fuzemeeting.com

Webinars are Internet based platforms that use powerpoint slides, video clips, whiteboards, and other auxiliary tools to conduct online meetings, workshops, presentations, and seminars. There are websites that offer free webinar hosting, however, most charge for their services. If you are a Mac user like I am. hosting webinars on certain services can be limiting. I have listed www.fruzmeeting.com because it accepts hosts who own older Macs, and it records the meetings as part of its package. There is a charge, but the overall quality of the webinar is excellent. I have used other webinar hosting services and will continue to look for companies that can improve on webinar capabilities.

I have conducted diversity webinars for nearly five years. They provide a cost effective method of distributing information to audiences around the world for a fraction of the cost of meeting face to face. You also have the option of collaborating with others if you are planning a project and want the participation of colleagues or new contact in other states or other countries.

My **Multicultural Symposium Series** (MSS) (www.mssconnect.com) offers a monthly workshop on a different topic to its members each month. The one hour webinar is recorded and then archived on my password protected web page afterward. Members are given a passcode and can retrieve each webinar on demand. It's convenient, cost effective and content rich for all who participate as members of MSS.

Chapter 19

Tip #18: Travel Outside Of Your Country At Least Once In Your Life

There is nothing like travel. It is by far the best way to expand your diversity and multicultural experience by putting you in direct contact with people who are different and similar to you. Here are some immediate diversity benefits from traveling to other countries:

--Meet people who are ethnically different and/or similar to you

--Meet people in their native land who speak a different language from you

--Eat different foods cook by the locals

--Experience a different political/governmental system

--Read different newspapers and magazines than your own

--See different housing structures that are similar or different from your own

--Talk to people who have specific opinions about their own country

--Talk to people who have opinions about your country

--Learn more about the work habits, hours, and regulations of that country

--Understand how religion either impacts or does not factor into society

--Experience the weather, the social customs, fashion, and traditions

This list could go on for several pages, but I hope you will think of other valid reasons why traveling outside of your country has its benefits.

Planning

I completely understand that some of you are reading this chapter and cannot feasibly travel anywhere for the foreseeable future. Perhaps you have just started a family, or your eldest child just started college, or you are the primary caregiver for your elderly parents. Or perhaps now is just not a financially stable time for you to explore international travel options.

If not now, plan for your trip for sometime in the future. It could be two years from now or ten years. Maybe you have to defer your travel plans until you retire in 15 years. The important point is to identify a part of the world that intrigues you and set a month and date that you want to get there. There is power in this form of goal setting, and if you write down the name of the country and the date and month you're planning for your visit, you increase your chances of actually achieving your goal.

Goal Setting

Anyone can wish upon a star that you'll reach your goal. It's more important to write it down and see it through, no matter how long it takes to get there.

In Chapter Eight I talked about the importance of creating a vision for yourself. For me, the vision statement that came flooding in my head during that turbulent time in my life in 1998 transformed my thinking. By that time I had traveled and worked in Canada, had worked in Australia, and had recently worked in England. Little did I realize that writing down the phrase: "**...purpose, courage, and faith to people throughout the world**," would take me to counties in Africa (Kenya and South Africa) and to El Salvador. My vision statement expanded my worldwide network and planted new seeds of connections to people I had only read about in books. Little did I realize that the advancement of technology would literally revolutionize the way I communicated and collaborated with people all over the world.

Saving

Your main focus in traveling should not be racking up the costs and overshooting your budget. Your goal is to plan for an affordable and enjoyable trip that won't leave you broke. There are countless banks in the United States that allow you to establish a savings or special account specifically designed for vacation travel. Your trip can also involve mission work to a distant country who will value you working with indigenous people who can use your support and assistance. You can also combine a vacation with mission work, as the Kenya Sistahs did with our 2005 and 2007 trips to Kenya. Again you have the freedom and flexibility to design your trip to satisfy your needs.

You can save money weekly, monthly or yearly...you decide how often you want to save for your trip and how much you need to save to get there.

For example, I want to visit India and would like to travel there within the next six years. I would budget $6000 for the trip, including airfare, hotel accommodations, meals and ground transportation. With over one billion people, India represents one of the most diverse countries in the world. I want to experience the depths of that diversity up close and personal. I would need to save $1000 a year for six years to reach my goal. That represents $20 a week, a reasonable weekly amount to save with that much advance planning.

You, too can determine how many years of planning you need, the estimated cost of your trip (overestimate this number) and then divide up that number into a weekly amount you'll need to save to underwrite the cost of the trip. Of course any windfall financial gift, income tax refund, or unexpected revenue could also cut the time of saving for your big trip.

Trips Around the World

Don't overlook a trip around the world that you can save for and experience. Don't laugh. I know of at least two people in my circle of colleagues who have taken that type of trip. It's not as expensive as you think, now that designated airlines will allow you to purchase one ticket that routes you in one direction, allowing stops along the way of your great adventure. Go to these websites for more information about trips around the world:

www.gobackpacking.com
www.lonelyplanet.com
www.nationalgeographicexpeditions.com
www.staralliance.com

Explore

This chapter is especially dedicated to my American friends who are reluctant to step off American soil. You in particular need to explore a different country before you die. Only 30% of Americans have a passport. I hope that this book will increase that percentage with avid learners who want to expand their appreciation of cultures beyond their borders.

Plan. Set Goals. Save. Consider a trip around the world. Explore other cultures. Most importantly, embrace the world wherever you live and develop a thirst for traveling beyond your normal. comfort zone. It is by far the best way to experience diversity and multiculturalism in real time. You owe it to yourself to expand your horizons and travel to another country sometime during your lifetime.

Chapter 20

Tip #19: Become A Mentor & Find An Accountability Partner

Your job as a multicultural advocate won't be complete until you reach out and touch the lives of other people. Leading and guiding others is the job of a mentor. Meeting the expectations you set for yourself requires an accountability partner or mastermind group.

These concepts serve different roles and should not be interpreted as functioning as the same. Let's take a look at their individual meanings.

Mentor

A mentor is a person who offers guidance, wisdom and support to an individual who is in a more junior position. A mentor can be a senior or "seasoned" person in an organization who commits to teaching or providing guidance to a person or "mentee" in a a more junior position within the same organization, industry, or a different one.

Career Mentoring

The goal of a mentor is to support the mentee in career or leadership development strategies. For example, my cousin, Jacquelyn Gaines, is one of the few African American women to have led two major hospital organizations in the United States. In fact very few women make it to the top of hospital administration. Early in Jackie's career as a nurse there were hospital executives who recognized her leadership potential and made themselves available to mentor her. She took their advice, earned an advance graduate degree to enhance her competitive edge, and was not afraid to relocate with her husband and family to other parts of the country as leadership posts became available. Her ability to leverage executive leadership roles was more than evident. However, the early guidance she received from mentors made the difference between Jackie finishing her career as a top nurse verses the hospital CEO that she became.

Youth Mentoring: Leaders Of Tomorrow

I have been a member of The National Black MBA Association (NBMBAA) for more than 25 years. (www.nbmbaa.org) I am a life member, have held many leadership positions, have hosted a national conference, and continue to have a deep affection for the organization. Friends like Dr. Earl Avery, Jeanne Leccese, Dr. Barbara Addison Reid, Linda Watters, Renee Malbranche and many others have been champions of the various local and national programs, scholarships, and projects managed by the organization each year.

The one program of which I am most proud is NBMBAA's Leaders of Tomorrow (LOT) initiative (LOT). Started in 1991 as a experimental program for minority middle and high school students, LOT has become a popular and successful testament to mentoring young adults by exposing them to the world of business. I am honored to have co-founded LOT and urged our local members to get involved when I served as the Boston Chapter President over 20 years ago.

Our local chapter was extremely fortunate to have dedicated and experienced adults who volunteered their time to work with LOT students year after year. Friends across the country including Dr. Jessica Henderson Daniel, Dr. Em Claire Knowles, Lois Graham, Loretta Gene and Elaine Munn mentored students on the local level and in LOT chapters in the United States and the UK. NBMBAA staff and board leadership were also essential for ensuring the success of the program. They included Antoinette Malveaux, Barbara Thomas,

Lisa Gene, Pamela Anderson, Beverly Harris, Audrey Hines and Bill Wells.

Alan Wade was the Boston Chapter's first LOT Director. He was highly recommended by his brother, Charles, who served as one of NBMBAA Chapter Presidents. For years Alan worked closely with Elaine Munn, taking the students to NBMBAA conferences and LOT events all over the United States. They mentored students, guided them, and advised them on subjects from how to write resumes to how to complete a college application. They remained in a team leadership role for nearly 15 years. And with their guidance, they developed a student leadership pipeline with several of their mentees. Two of their LOT students, Gary Morton and Rabby Bristol not only graduated from high school, but finished college, married, started families, and remain active as alumni of LOT. Today, Gary, Rabby and other LOT alum, including Hamel Husbands and Dante Cunningham run the program! It speaks to the power and the long lasting impact of mentoring.

Accountability Partner
An accountability partner is a colleague, co-worker, friend, family member or acquaintance who commits to supporting your efforts in achieving personal and/or professional success in exchange for you supporting their efforts. The person is of equal standing to you, is your peer, and is as interested in getting support from you as they are in supporting your game plan. It's an equal partnership, a shared relationship, and collaboration where you encourage each other in your respective paths to success.

For nearly five years, professional speaker and colleague Robin Thompson was my accountability partner. We met as members of the National Speakers Association during one of our national conventions. I am African American. She is

White. I lived in Massachusetts. She and her husband were relocating from Utah back to their native West Virginia.

Robin and I dutifully set up regular 90 minute conference call meetings each month that provided an opportunity to gauge how well our respective speaking and training activities were going. We shared our goals with each other and held each other accountable. I owe a debt of gratitude to Robin for holding me to task to complete and publish my book, Personal Empowerment, How To Turbo Charge Your Life Both On And Off Your Job. She held me accountable through the book's completion, through it's debut, and throughout the many book signings I had nearly a decade ago.

I held Robin accountable as she launched new training programs, started a line of greeting cards featuring her beautiful photographs of the West Virginia countryside, and urged her on as she because an early adapter of internet marketing initiatives.

Our ethnic backgrounds were very different, but that probably helped to sustain our accountability partnership for that extended length of time. Our peer relationship was a plus, and helped me to support a friend and colleague who was different yet very similar to my own background.

Mastermind Group

A mastermind group is very similar to an accountability partner. You just have more people involved in the process. Each member of the group is a peer in either the same industry, organization or profession. Regular meetings are established, either face to face or by phone. Membership is determined by the group itself. It's either open to select participants or is closed by mutual agreement of the group at large. The purpose of the group is to support the activities of each member as each person strives for career, business or professional success. Each member shares in the management of the group, usually by taking turns in planning meeting schedules and other responsibilities related to the sustainability of the group's survival. Like other group dynamics, personality strengths, weaknesses and conflicts can influence the overall viability of the group's long term outcome.

I have belonged to several mastermind groups in the past 15 years. Some were successful, while others were not. For nearly six years I have been a member of **"Ebony Speakers,"** a mastermind group I co-founded with three other African American professional speakers. We all met through the National Speakers Association and have have been in business for roughly the same number of years. (www.ebonyspeakers.com)

Although we are all Black women, our differences, similarities and common faith traditions bind us together. **Debra Washington Gould** lives and works in New Orleans, and has secured large government contracts through her firm. **Nancy Lewis** lives and works in Atlanta and is one of the most innovative marketing professionals that I know. **Michelle Portia** lives in Connecticut and spent several years working for HBO before transitioning into her business full time. She has successfully tapped into the youth market and frequently delivers her training programs to that audience.

We meet monthly by phone for at least one hour. We share in the responsibility of managing and scheduling our meetings, rotating quarterly with who will lead the group. We have met face to face on several occasions, and have twice supported and participated in Nancy's women's conferences in Atlanta. The group supported the initial launch of the Multicultural Symposium Series when my conference series debuted in 2008.

We are all Christians, and open and close all of our meetings in prayer. Our faith has been a long lasting bond and has helped to strengthen us during difficult times. We intend to publish a book together in the near future, and look forward to continuing our accountability to each other well into the foreseeable future.

Relationship Building, Diversity, Mentorship, Accountability, and Mastermind Achievements.

The type of relationship you identify depends on how diversity factors into your professional plan of action. If you are a human resource manager with important corporate responsibilities, you can serve as a mentor to a junior colleague in your company or your trade organization. You can also identify a trusted accountability partner who can support your efforts during times of opportunity or when you're surrounded by challenges. Or perhaps a mastermind group of like minded HR professionals is the best route for you as you continue to build your professional career.

No matter what your occupation, profession or career path, your diversity journey can definitely expand through mentorship, finding an accountability partner or joining a mastermind group. Determine what your needs are and explore new diversity and multicultural opportunities through relationships built on trust and respect.

Chapter 21

Tip #20: Learn More About Religion: Your Own and Others

"Almost every story around the world has a religion sub-plot."
--Bruce Buursma

Religion, faith based initiatives, or the lack of religion are volatile polarizing topics that most diversity professionals like to avoid. I do not avoid these topics. I embrace them. I believe that understanding religion is one of the core foundations of diversity training and should be embraced more openly. It can be controversial if approached with little regard for an opposing belief. Religion has certainly been the cause of warfare, torture, genocide and unthinkable violence throughout the ages, and can cause great harm if oppressively imposed on communities strongly rooted in their own faith based initiatives.

Despite the emotional touchstone, real diversity advocates should study and expand their knowledge of various religious ideologies.

I am a strong believer in the separation of church and state. I don't feel that it's appropriate for one religious group to oppress, conquer, and control simply in the name of a higher power. However, I am a deeply religious person, am an officer in my church, and pray constantly. I also respect other religious beliefs and will spend the remainder of my life learning about my own religion and that of others. Perhaps it's because I come from a long line of ministers in the African Methodist Episcopal Church and was married to one for nearly twenty years. Religion is a central theme in my life; yet I have so much more to learn.

Sometimes Religious Training Kicks In Automatically - September 11th

There are some unscripted life events that make it impossible to partition religious practices from daily activities. Because I am a diversity professional I usually curtail my own religious beliefs and practices from the workplace. I can also modify my traditions, such as bowing my head and silently saying my "table grace" at a public meal function. I also refrain from expressing my personal religious viewpoints when I am conducting my diversity sessions or consulting with clients related to my business activities.

All of those restraints disappeared on September 11, 2001. That morning I was conducting a training session for 125 women working at Verizon, the giant telecommunication company. A large percentage of the women were physically seated in my session in downtown Boston. The rest were watching remotely in different locations across the region. When the first plane hit the World Trade Center, two officials quietly entered the room and waited for me to pause my presentation. I thought something had happened within the company, and an announcement needed to be made. They quietly walked over to me and whispered what had happened. It was truly a surreal moment, causing me not to panic or show any signs of anxiety because all of the women were watching me. I quietly let them know what was going on in New York and asked that we pause for a moment of silent prayer for those impacted by the tragedy. I knew the situation was grave and that lives had been lost. Something inside of me automatically kicked into "prayer mode." There was nothing I could do to stop it.

A few moments later we resumed the training session, even though I had an uneasy feeling that the tragedy in New York was far from over. Minutes later the officials returned to the room and urgently came to me with terrible news. A second plane had crashed into the World Trade Center and it was advised that we end the session. That was when I had to suppress a panic attack. You see the planes had originated from Boston's Logan airport, I was working in a large high rise building for a major telecommunications company in downtown Boston, and we had no way of knowing if our city would soon be attacked next. I asked everyone to remain calm, to pray, and to stay safe.

Internet reception inside of the building was difficult at best. My cell phone would not work, because the circuits were overloaded. By the time I left the building, the streets were jammed with people. Very scared people. I was worried about my niece, Lauren Copeland, who was a graduate student in New York. Fortunately she was unharmed and a good distance away from the Twin Towers. My own daughters were out of harm's way in Chicago and Connecticut. My mind raced back and forth, and my internal prayers intensified. What was going on???? Who was responsible for these terrible acts??? Was Boston next on the list????

Instinct kept kicking in and I rode the crowded subway back to get my car and drove straight to the radio station, WILD-1090 AM. I had hosted a radio program there for nearly two years and felt compelled to go to the station to help inform the general public what was going on. I ended up going on the air with another colleague, and we stayed on the radio live until the end of the broadcasting day, around 6 pm. We played ABC news feeds, talked to callers, and asked questions about a name that kept popping up-Osama bin Laden. I later learned that my friends, Elda and Maurice Wright were on vacation on Cape Cod, had no television, but were listening intently to every word we were saying on the radio. We also learned that a third plane hit its mark and crashed into the Pentagon in Washington DC. A fourth hijacked plane, bound for Washington, met resistance from passengers onboard who successfully aborted the mission by crashing the plane in a rural region in Pennsylvania.

The saga continued for me on September 12th, the day I was scheduled to conduct a leadership training retreat for executives at the TJX Companies. Driving to that session left me in tears. When I arrived, I was not the only one crying. We could not hold the session because it was just too painful for anyone to concentrate. The company had lost seven employees on one of the planes that had crashed into the World Trade Center. The attendees at the retreat were inconsolable. They asked me questions I could not answer. All I could do was ask them to remain in prayer, for the victims, for the loved ones left behind and for themselves and the other employees whose collective grief could not be measured.

I later learned that one employee from Verizon had also been killed on September 11th. I was told that the calm, prayerful sprit of that morning training session comforted some of the women who lost their colleagues during the terrorist attacks.

The horrific experiences of September 11th illustrate the difficulty of strict separation of church and state. Christianity, Islam, Judaism, and many of the other world religions were in plain sight that day when nearly 3000 citizens of all ethnicities and religions perished at the hands of madmen. I was unable to separate my faith from the tragedies of my business clients. That day reminded me that sometimes life calls up your religious beliefs and demands that they get used to comfort the agony and suffering in your midst.

Major Religions Of The World
No two lists are the same, and how official religious groups are counted determine the total numbers of each sect. With that disclaimer, here is a list of the top religious groups in the world:

World Religions
2.1 billion	Christianity
1.5 billion	Islam
1.1 billion	Secular/Non Religious/Agnostic/Atheist
900 million	Hinduism
394 million	Chinese Traditional Religion
376 million	Buddhism
300 million	Primal-indigenous
100 million	African Traditional & Diasporic
23 million	Sikhism
14 million	Judaism

Source: www.adherents.com and www.religioustolerence.org

Religion In The United States
78.4% of Americans identify themselves as Christian.
Other Religion (Jewish Conservative & Orthodox): 4.7%
Buddhist: .7%
Muslim: .6%
Hindu: .4%
Non Religious: 16.1%
Source: Pew Research Study on Religion In America

Sources These Lists And For Other Facts About Religion
www.religioustolerance.org
I have been a strong supporter of www.religioustolerance.org since it started in 1995. Based in Canada, the website provides some of the most comprehensive, non judgmental information on most of the world's religions from Christianity to Wicca. The website's goal is to educate the general public

about the world religions without proselytizing. Their profiles on the different religious groups provide enough background materials for you to launch other your own search for truth, meaning and purpose.

www.adherents.com

This website provides a comprehensive collection of data, information and top ten lists from most of world religions. The list of world religions included in this chapter originated from this website. I suggest that you combine your research from www.religioustolerance.org with www.adherents.com to validate your information for credibility and accuracy.

Pew Research Center, Washington DC
www.pewresearch.org

The Pew Research Center is a nonpartisan fact tank that provides information on the issues, attitudes and trends shaping America and the world. The center conducts public opinion polling, demographic studies, media content analysis and other empirical social science research. It does not take positions on policy issues. The Pew Center has extensive data on religious activities in the United States.

10 Ways To Explore Diversity Advocacy Through Religious Research

1. Understand that religion plays a direct or indirect role in how most societies function.
2. Become a "chief learning officer" of your own religion before judging others.
3. Visit the faith based activities and services of religions other than your own.
4. Ask questions about dress restrictions, food preparation and other policies before visiting a religious service different from your own.
5. Visit www.youtube.com to watch other religious traditions different from your own.

6. Watch your own display of religious practices unless extreme world events like September 11th call for them to be used to comfort others.

7. Examine your own concept of the separation of church and state.

8. Don't forget that respect for all humanity is always welcomed regardless of your personal religious beliefs.

9. Check with your employer before establishing a religious small group session at work
(This would also apply to creating a prayer room for Muslims who pray five times a day).

10. Remember you don't have all the answers, but you do have the ability to learn about world religions and how they affect us all.

Chapter 22

Tip #21: Speak Up, Stand Out, Become A Diversity Champion

"Just as Socrates felt that it was necessary to create a tension in the mind so that individuals could rise from the bondage of myths and half-truths to the unfettered realm of creative analysis and objective appraisal, so must we see the need for nonviolent gadflies to create the kind of tension in society that will help men rise from the dark depths of prejudice and racism to the majestic heights of understanding and brotherhood."

--Dr. Martin Luther King, Jr.
Letter From A Birmingham Jail
April 16, 1963

It takes courage and bravery to stand up for justice, equality, diversity and multiculturalism. I thought many years ago that my life's work would take me to easier pastures, less difficult terrain, and working with more user friendly subject matters. Thinking back on that undergraduate degree I earned from Emory University in 1975 and that MBA degree I took home from Northeastern University in 1985, I imagined a charmed life filled with endless opportunities to succeed with ease. Instead the ups and downs of my personal journey have strengthened and stressed me through five decades on this planet. As the great Langston Hughes said, "Life for me ain't been no crystal stair."

The journey as a global diversity advocate and small business owner has been filled with great joys and very deep sorrows. I could paper my wall ten times over with the "NOs" I have routinely received, the unreturned phone calls and the routine rejections from prospective clients always waiting for me around the corner. The challenges and difficulties could make me cry; yet they merely fortify me to press forward, move beyond the barriers, and find new ways to get my message heard.

I am a pioneer business leader and no stranger to personal difficulties. I am also a survivor and use my mistakes, failures, challenges, and bad breaks to mount new efforts to become a better global thought leader. I believe in transparency and "seamless living," where your message and image follow you wherever you go. And in the words of Dr. Martin Luther King, Jr, I am looking for more pioneer "gadflies" to make this world a better place for us all.

I am looking for people like you to Stand Up, Speak Out and become a Diversity Champion.

What is a Diversity Champion?

A diversity champion is a person who stands up for truth, respects the dignity of people from all walks of life and realizes that their personal point of view might be different from other people. In the United States a diversity champion votes in EVERY election and pays attention to local, state, national and international issues beyond the sound bytes of a TV talk show.

A diversity champion is a curious lifelong learner. Diversity champions aren't afraid of failure and understands that the route to long term achievement is often traveled through roads of failure,disappointments, setbacks and challenges. The quest for knowledge is so great that the diversity challenger will sacrifice time and money to expand their storehouse of wisdom and knowledge.

I look at my treasured friend and mentor Juanita Abernathy as not only a civil rights legend but also a diversity champion.

She is the widow of Dr. Ralph David Abernathy, who was the closest associate to Dr. Martin Luther King, Jr. Her legacy includes a mixture of standing for justice and equality with her husband when it was safer and more popular to silently accept America the way it was. And even though her husband died more than twenty years ago, she remains an active diversity champion for women and people of color throughout the world.

A diversity champion knows they don't have all of the answers. In fact they might not have many answers at all. However, the diversity champion understands that patience and persistence are the steady forces that ultimately lead to greater awareness and useful dialogue with diverse people.

Diversity champions are not perfect people. They are just like you and me, flawed, overwhelmed at times, but striving to live a descent life by peacefully coexisting with others.

Diversity champions deeply care about their families, their communities, their friends and their colleagues.

There simply aren't enough diversity champions in the world. It is my hope and prayer that you will join the brigade and advocate for diversity and multiculturalism wherever you go.

10 Ways To Become A Diversity Champion In The United States

1. **VOTE in ALL elections in your town.** Voting every four years for presidential candidates is only part of the voting process. Vote in every single village, town, city, state and national election.

2. Don't laugh when someone tells racist jokes. It your own style, suggest to that person that the joke really isn't appropriate to tell in public or private.

3. Stop being so scared to take action at work. Remember the sacrifices of those during the civil rights era who marched, joined boycotts, and put their jobs on the line so that others could taste freedom and equality. When you see injustice on the job, say something.

4. Yes one vote does matter. Your vote matters. There are countless examples where the difference between victory and defeat rested in a handful of a few votes.

5. Buy a second copy of this book, give it to someone who doesn't believe in diversity and start a discussion group about the real impact of diversity both on and off the job.

6. Attend public hearings in your local community and keep abreast of the issues in our region. Diversity has everything to do with politics. And everyone is affected by politics.

7. Stop behaving like you have no power. You have power and influence in many ways, and it's up to you to demonstrate it when you interact with people who are similar and different from you.

8. Don't be afraid to debate others on key issues. Many people spout out ideas and opinions that are simply baseless and not grounded in facts. This applies to some information espoused by talk show hosts and political pundits. Research the correct information and engage in a friendly debate with those who could benefit from your insight.

9. Remember that you are a role model to someone on your job. There is someone on your job who admires you and wants to be just like you. Demonstrate your respect for diversity and multiculturalism with everyone you meet both on and off your job.

10. **You are a global citizen. Lead by example.** Stand up for truth. Stand up for others. Connect with the rest of the world on your job, in your community, with your colleagues, and online.

About The Author

As a speaker, trainer, global thought leader, and business owner since 1987, **Carole Copeland Thomas** moderates the discussions of key issues affecting our global marketplace. She has her pulse on the issues affecting working professionals and consults with industry leaders on a regular basis. From speaking at the Federal Highway Administration, SHRM, Hewlett Packard, Verizon, Cargill, and Monster.com to interviewing experts around the globe, Carole knows how to analyze the dynamics of a changing marketplace.

Outreach To Global Issues
Carole served as an adjunct faculty member for Bentley University for a decade, and has spoken throughout the United States, London, England, Canada, El Salvador, Australia, South Africa, and Kenya. She recently co-founded a non-profit international organization with nine other women as a result of a 2005 trip to Kenya. The group returned to Kenya in November 2007 for humanitarian projects and to host their first International   Conference in Mombasa, Kenya.

Author
Carole is the author of two books, including her new book: Best Practices: 21 Ways To Bring Multiculturalism To Your Job Your Home and Your Community.

Multicultural Symposium Series
Carole is the founder of the Multicultural Symposium Series, a multiyear conference and online initiative developed for the advancement of multicultural issues. Carole is a blogger and social media enthusiast using various technology platforms to enhance her business development activities.

Radio Talk Show & Executive Coach
Carole is the host of Focus On Empowerment a weekly issues-oriented radio talk show. The program recently migrated to Internet radio on Blog Talk Radio. www.blogtalkradio.com/globalcarole

For three years Carole's Personal Empowerment Tips were heard daily on Boston's WILD 1090 AM Radio. Her one-hour call in radio talk show, "Focus On Empowerment" was heard every Friday morning on the station. Carole's syndicated radio tips were broadcast in 10 US cities in early 2003, and were sponsored by Marshalls the nationwide off-price retail store. Her radio talk show continued on WBNW-1120-AM-Boston through 2009. Carole served as the Executive Coach for the Essence Magazine Leadership Summit.

State & National Elections
Carole, a three-time state convention delegate, served as a town coordinator in the November 2006 successful election of Deval Patrick, Massachusetts' first African American governor. She also served as an active tri-state volunteer for the 2008 campaign of President Barack Obama.

Active In Community and Civic Affairs
Carole is the Tri State Coordinator for Delta Sigma Theta Sorority and the Chair of the Multicultural Committee for the Greater Boston Convention and Visitors Bureau. A lifetime member of the National Black MBA Association, Carole served as Past President of the Boston Chapter and Past National Vice Chair of the organization.

Education
Carole graduated with honors in 1975 from Emory University. She entered graduate school in 1983 (on a Martin Luther King, Jr. academic fellowship), and received her MBA degree from Northeastern University in Boston.

Mother and Grandmother
Carole is the mother of three children: Dr. Lorna Thomas Farquharson (husband Jerome), Michelle Thomas, and the late Mickarl D. Thomas, Jr. She does her best to spoil her granddaughters Julianna Gwendolyn Farquharson and Gabrielle Jaeda Farquharson.

Professional
Speaking Services

For your next convention, conference, meeting,
workshop, retreat, or staff session you can
count on the speaking services of
Carole Copeland Thomas.

Specializing in global diversity, multiculturalism,
empowerment, leadership, youth and women's issues,
Carole's message will leave a lasting impression
with your audience.

To Book Carole, Contact Her At:

(508) 947-5755 - Office

(508) 947-3903 - Fax

carole@mssconnect.com - email

Sign Up For Carole's Online Newsletter at

www.tellcarole.com

or

www.mssconnect.com

Speaking • Training • Consulting• Facilitation

The Multicultural Symposium
SERIES
Membership Open To ANYONE
IN THE WORLD!

MULTICULTURAL
Symposium Series
www.mssconnect.com

Webinars • Conferences • E Newsletters • Discounts
Face To Face • Online • On The Air

MEMBERSHIP FORM

Name (Please Print)

Organization

Address   Suite/Apt#

City   State   Zip

Daytime Phone   Home Phone

Email Address   Date of Birth (Month/Day)

Payment Method

_____Money Order _____Check _____AMEX _____Visa _____Mastercard

_____Membership(s) at $99 each   _____

TOTAL PAYMENT   _____

Credit Card Number   Exp Date

Credit Card Billing Address   3-4 Digit Security Code

www.mssconnect.com • Email: carole@mssconnect.com

Please clip and mail to: C. Thomas & Associates
6 Azel Road, Lakeville, Massachusetts 02347
Questions??Call Carole at (508) 947-5755

Best Practices
21 Ways
TO BRING MULTICULTURALISM
TO YOUR JOB YOUR HOME
and
YOUR COMMUNITY

A Practical Guide To Global Diversity

ORDER FORM

Name (Please Print)

Organization

Shipping Address   Suite/Apt#

City   State   Zip

Daytime Phone   Home Phone

Email Address

Payment Method

_____Money Order _____Check _____AMEX _____Visa _____Mastercard

Send _____books at $15 each   _____   **Shipping & Handling**

+% Sales Tax (MA Residents Only)   _____   **$5 for the 1st book**

TOTAL PAYMENT   _____   **$2 for each additional book**

Credit Card Number   Exp Date

Credit Card Billing Address   3-4 Digit Security Code

www.mssconnect.com • Email: carole@mssconnect.com

Please clip and mail to: C. Thomas & Associates

6 Azel Road, Lakeville, Massachusetts 02347

For Bulk Orders and Special Discount Pricing Call Carole at (508) 947-5755

Praise For Best Practices 21 Ways

An absolute must read. Copeland Thomas masterfully enlightens and educates with a straightforward framework designed to produce positive results for families, community groups and corporations. <u>21 Steps</u>, a roadmap to achieving success through inclusiveness and open-mindedness, is simply superb!

"Everyone wants to transform, but nobody wants to change" Fredrica Mattewes-Green

Linda A. Watters, Vice President – Government Relations, John Hancock Financial Services, Boston

Who better than Carole Copeland Thomas to capture in easy steps the practices and procedures necessary to guide individuals and companies toward a better understanding of the current principles of multiculturalism and diversity? This book explains in simple terms some best practices, while emphasizing the critical role leadership plays in helping to successfully implement new strategies.

Dr. Carole A. Cowan, President
Middlesex Community College

Carole brings exceptional insight and real-life experience to her writing on multiculturalism. Her knowledge – influenced strongly by a family history of community service and faith – is based in genuine respect for all people and all cultures. She does not just write about her beliefs, she lives them with style, panache and grace. This book is a "must-read" for anyone who accepts that multiculturalism is not an option, but a requirement for survival in today's world.

Denise Gray-Felder, President and CEO
Communication for Social Change Consortium www.cfsc.org

If you want to cut through the jargon and push past the slogans, this is your book. If you want to get to the real meat of making our differences (and similarities) assets, instead of liabilities, a source of strength, instead of weakness, and an opportunity for enrichment, instead of conflict, this is your book. If you're as hungry as I am for a life full of relationships with "all of God's children", this is your book. Read it, enjoy it, and then do it.

Rev. Ray Hammond
Senior Pastor
Bethel African Methodist Episcopal Church
Boston

As globalisation becomes more and more important in all countries and communities of our shrinking world, it also becomes ever more important to embrace the immense benefits of multiculturalism and diversity, thus releasing the many talents of so many of our citizens. '21 Ways to Bring Multiculturalism to Your Job, Your Home, & Your Community' provides plentiful insights and a rich range of challenges by an author who is a true expert in this dynamic and increasingly pivotal industry. This is a book from the heart which should be read carefully and thoughtfully. Hugely to be recommended

**Garth Dallas, CEO at Global Diversity Partners Ltd,
Editor at Diverse Magazine Liverpool, England**

Carole Copeland Thomas brings the discussion around multiculturalism and diversity to a level anyone can wrap their brain and heart around. She brings the reader on a journey of reality and opportunity. This is worth the read and offers lots of conversation stimulators.

**Georgianna Meléndez
Executive Director
Commonwealth Compact**